A World of Costumes in cutout

A World of

Costumes in cutout

written and designed by
Rosemary Lowndes and Claude Kaïler
for Holt, Rinehart and Winston·New York

How to use this book

This book will make up into your own gallery of fashion. By simply cutting out the pages you will have :
9 three dimensional costume models 20cm (8") high ready to cut out, fold and glue, together with easy to follow visual instructions.
9 fashion plates to cut out and frame or pin up on a wall.
A complete illustrated booklet of costume through the ages to cut out and bind, which can be used as a descriptive guide for each model.

GENERAL INSTRUCTIONS FOR MAKING THE MODELS

You will need :
Good sharp scissors
A tube of transparent glue
Some cardboard for mounting the backgrounds
Time and patience

Remember always to :
Cut along black lines
Fold these lines outwards
Fold these lines inwards
Glue these areas

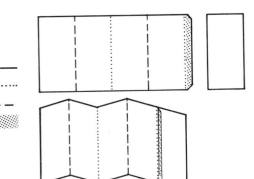

IMPORTANT

When you have cut out the pieces place them the right side up on a table on a sheet of paper so as not to lose them.
Fold and bend the pieces carefully following the assembly order as shown by the photographs and make sure that you have got the shapes and folds correct before finally glueing them in place.
If you have difficulty glueing tubular pieces such as necks, it is a good idea to roll them around a pencil whilst glueing them in shape. Then use the pencil or scissors to push the glue covered flanges up inside the neck afterwards.
Make the model first, then cut out the background carefully leaving the fashion plates and booklet till the end.

HOW TO MOUNT THE BACKGROUNDS so they stand up behind each model.
Paste each background onto a piece of stiff cardboard cut to the same size, cut another piece of cardboard into a wedge shape. Fold it in half, glue one half to the back as shown on the photograph.
When you have made up the models and their backgrounds, turn to the last page of the book for instructions and ideas on how to make the booklet and display the fashion plates.

LC: 77-73858
ISBN : 0-03-020936-6

10 9 8 7 6 5 4 3 2 1

Printed in Great Britain

EGYPTIAN   GREEK   ROMAN   BYZANTINE

1230   1350   1410   1460

BURGUNDIAN

1   Nature had failed to protect early man with abundant fur which meant that he was forced to kill wild animals for their coats to keep himself warm. Because he was a hunter the hides he used had to be shaped to give him freedom of movement.

With the passage of time he found that fleece could be clipped, spun and woven on a loom. This was the beginning of cloth as we know it today. As the Assyrian, Babylonian, Egyptian and Greek civilizations progressed, they draped and folded the cloth, and gave certain styles to each individual ; be it man or woman, slave or master, high priest or king. Wars between nations forced the vanquished to wear the fashions of the victors, so that when the Romans created an empire throughout Europe and North Africa they introduced their own style of clothing but also adopted the garments of the people whom they had conquered. Influenced by the Gauls and Celts they shortened their togas and began to wear a version of knee length trousers.

In the twelfth century Christian Knights from all over Europe banded together to repel the hordes of Moslems who had overrun the Christian countries of the Near East. These crusaders not only returned home with wealth and power, but in their travels extended their knowledge of other peoples and cultures, including a new style of Gothic architecture. The soaring pointed Gothic arch replaced the simple rounded Roman arch ; buildings were high and narrow ; the clothes copied the architecture, and it became fashionable for ladies to look tall and slender.

The men of the thirteenth century wore long belted robes called 'surcotes' over their under tunics, short breeches and long hose (or stockings). Their cloaks were fastened at the front, or on the shoulder, by brooches, and the women wore similar gowns and cloaks.   In the fourteenth century a parti-coloured tunic called the cotehardie, with a

hooded shoulder cape became fashionable for men; a decorated belt was slung on the hips, and the women wore tight fitting cotehardies under loose, sideless surcotes.

By the early fifteenth century clothes were decorated by fluttering leaf shapes called 'daggings' cut out from the edges of the sleeves and tunics.

The fourteenth and fifteenth centuries, in spite of long and almost continuous wars, were years of adventure and riches for the nobles. During the fifteenth century the Princes of the proud state of Burgundy lived in magnificent wealth and extravagance. No expense was spared on clothing and fabrics. Rich velvets, soft silks, heavy damasks and shimmering satins, combined with precious jewels, added beauty and splendour to the age of chivalry. A courtier's head was easily turned by the elegance and loveliness of ladies dresses. Vanity and admiration caused exaggeration and gowns trailed, sleeves flowed from the arms, and headdresses became huge towering structures.

The most flattering woman's dress of this period was the 'houppelande' gown. This was high waisted, worn with a broad belt below the breast. Usually decorated with circles, stars or flower designs, the belt was thought to have magical powers. The low-cut neckline of the gown was filled in with a 'modesty' vest and it was considered improper for a woman to display her bare arms. So the sleeve was made long and tight, with fur-trimmed cuffs either worn folded down to cover half the hand, or else folded back over the wrist. The sleeve was so narrow that it had to be fastened with small buttons.

The skirt of the gown was full, and edged with fur, forming a long train which swept the ground at the back, and fell only a little shorter at the front and sides. In order to walk, a lady had to hold up the voluminous folds of her skirts, clasping them under her breast, with her head drooping forward, her shoulders back, bottom tucked in and her stomach pushed out which gave the medieval woman the peculiar pregnant look fashionable at the time. Her shoes were flat, so to make her look taller she wore a high cone-shaped headdress called the 'hennin' which could reach heights of 90 centimetres (three feet) or more. The hennin, worn far back on the head, was stiffened and covered in silver or gold brocade, or silk, sometimes bordered in velvet and topped by a delicate, floating transparent veil, which was shaped and wired into two or three wings. Fashion demanded that no hair should show beneath the headdress so women removed their eyebrows and the hair from the nape of their necks and foreheads.

A version of the houppelande was worn by men, but unlike those of the ladies did not reach the ground. By the middle of the fifteenth century however, the very short tunic became popular for younger men. The body of the tunic was padded, with flat pleats which came together at the waist and then flared out in the short skirt, sometimes edged with fur. The shoulders were padded and puffed out to add to the overall impression of slim waist and broad masculine chest and shoulders. The round, or slightly square neckline showed the collar of the 'undertunic'. Sleeves were often cut with an opening at elbow level to push the arms through, (showing off the decorative patterns of the undertunic) and allowing the rest of the sleeve to hang free. With the short tunic were worn hose, tailored of wool or cotton in various colours. These were close fitting, cut to the shape of the leg and tied at the waist.

Shoes were normally made of soft leather, but velvet, brocade and other materials were also used. Styles of men's shoes varied from decorated short boots, laced or buckled at the side, to snug-fitting shoes with very long pointed toes turned up at the end. So lengthy and impractical were the points of the shoes—sometimes reaching a length of 45 centimetres (eighteen inches)—that it became necessary to tie the end back onto the shoe. This rather absurd fashion went to such extremes that a law was eventually passed fining any man wearing shoes with points longer than 5 centimetres (two inches).

Most men throughout this period were clean-shaven with their hair cut at collar length and brushed down, with the ends turned in and curled under.

Jewelled neck chains were worn over the tunics; purses and daggers with decorated hilts were slung from the belts adding to the romantic splendours of the costumes.

With the lavish elegance of the court of Burgundy the excitement of wearing something new and different launched costume amongst the ruling classes into the beginning of a continuous chain of changing fashion.

1460

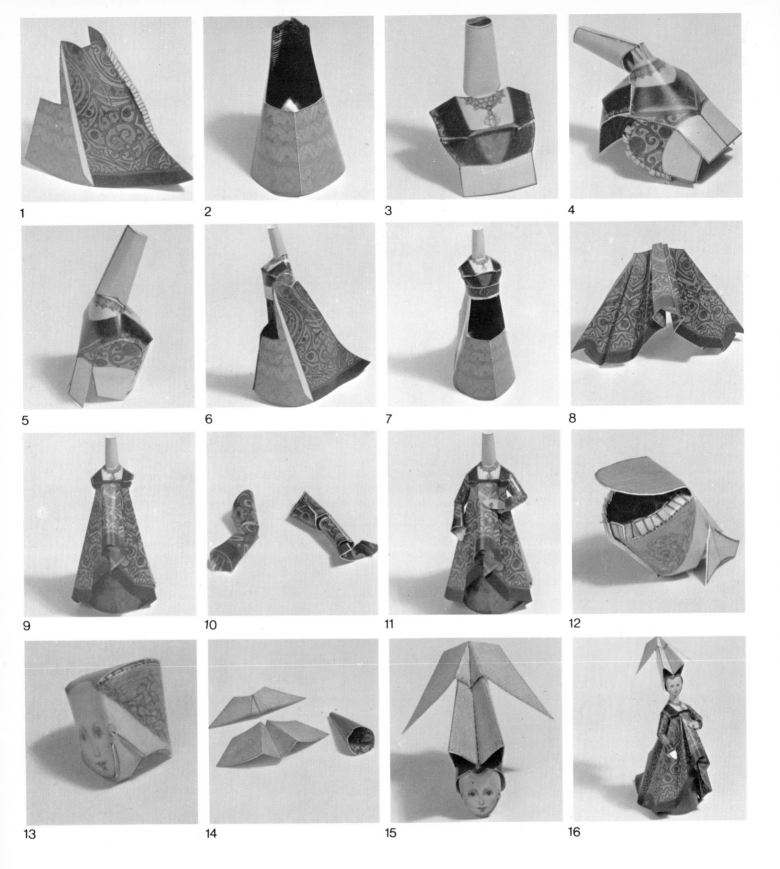

1
2
3
4
5
6
7
8
9
10
11
12
13
14
15
16

On the next two pages you will find a costume model of 1460
Cut out the pages carefully along the cutting lines.
When making the model it is important to follow the assembly
order by numbers as shown above.

For general instructions on cutting, folding and glueing see
page 4.

On the back of the cutout pages there are patchwork patterns.
These form the patterned linings to the dresses, hats and ribbons etc.

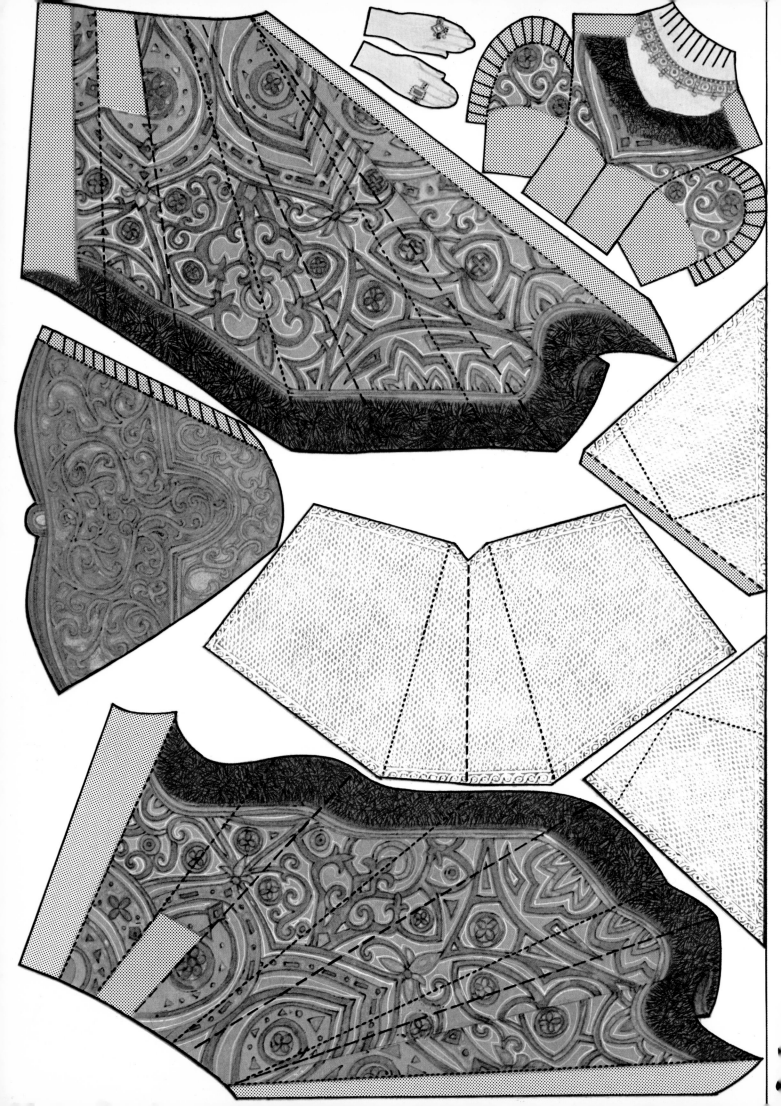

1500 ITALY

1515 GERMANY   1545 SPAIN   1540 GERMANY

1570 SPAIN   1570 FRANCE   1590 FRANCE

2   The end of the Medieval period heralded the start of Italian Renaissance fashions. Instead of the towering hennins of previous years, headdresses became lower and flatter. Sleeves grew larger and wider, and were detachable. The gowns were made of separate skirts and bodices sewn together at the waist opening on to under-skirts of great beauty. Women's necklines became square and the men's neckline lower, shoes were broad and as short as the foot instead of long and pointed. Men began to wear breeches and a curious German fashion called 'slashing' became popular. This consisted of pulling a vividly coloured contrasting lining through slits in the outer material of sleeves, doublet, and breeches. The male shirt became visible, eventually developing into a finely pleated affair worn under the doublet ending in a standing collar gathered in a small frill at the neck.

The flamboyant German influence of men's clothes with huge padded shoulders and lavish doublets in brilliant colours, hanging to the knee, gave way to the tight-laced, proud bearing and sombre colours of the Spanish court.

With the discovery of America, gold and precious stones poured into Spain, the wealthy, anxious to show off their new riches, encrusted their clothes with jewels—as safe a place as any to parade them as no banks existed. The ladies of fashion throughout Europe wore these richly embroidered fabrics tightly stretched over their bodices and hanging to the ground over cone-shaped Spanish farthingales which were made of canvas stiffened by hoops of wood or whalebone.

Later the French farthingale was introduced. This was either an enormous stuffed bolster called a 'bum-roll' tied below the waist, or a wheel of radiating spokes made of whalebone. These were worn under the skirt making the fabric spring out at the hip by as much as 60 centimetres (two feet) all the way round before dropping sharply to the ground.

To hide the hard line of the wheel or bum-roll a circular frill, called a flounce, was added. The hole for the waist was nearer the front of the skirt so that the wider portion at the back sloped upwards. To overcome the problem of sitting down comfortably a special farthingale chair was made.

Down the front of the bodice ending in a long point below the waist a piece of material called the 'stomacher' was pinned or laced. Heavily padded sleeves with tight wrist bands were tied on with ribbons or laces at the shoulders and armpits, with false hanging sleeves attached under the small 'wings' on the shoulders of the dress. The sleeves and stomachers were interchangeable so that they provided the wearer with different colour schemes in contrast to the overgown.

Cruel corsets enforced the rigid pose shown in paintings and portraits of the time. At first they were made of wooden laths held together by tapes and then metal corsets hinged at one side, padded and covered in velvet. These machines of torture rubbed the skin raw as they squeezed the flesh into the required stiff shape of tiny waist and flat bosom. Even children wore the same formal dresses and corsets as their parents ; hardly surprising, as at the age of thirteen a girl from a wealthy family was considered ready to marry and take on the responsibilities of a husband and household, having mastered the difficulties of Latin, tapestry and embroidery together with an appreciation of art and music which she had learnt from tutors at home. Her prowess at sewing would have been helpful, for men and women spent large sums of money on clothes.

Ruffs, which had begun as a small frill round the neck of the shirt developed into huge status symbols, proving by their size that the wearer was not involved in manual work. Some were so wide that eating was difficult and spoons with extra long handles had to be made so that food could be conveyed safely from plate to mouth. The ruffs were made of cambric decorated by lace edgings shaped by heated metal setting sticks and stiffened by wires and starch paste. Unmarried ladies wore heart-shaped ruffs and the married ones wore circular cartwheel ruffs.

Because of the elaborate ruffs it was now necessary for ladies to pile the hair on top of their heads, either turned back from the face over a pad or brushed over a high wired support, the back hair coiled or plaited was generally hidden by a jewelled hair net. Hair was dyed, often with disastrous results ; and wigs and false hair pieces were worn to cover the baldness caused by the use of dangerous concoctions of herbs and chemicals. Ladies painted their faces and bosoms with white powdered lead, and tinted their cheeks with vermilion to give a fashionable pink and white complexion and also to disguise blemishes and pock marks caused by smallpox and other diseases. The poisonous lead caused the early death of many vain women.

Men also wore large ruffs and make-up for them was not unusual, they also put oil and pomade on their faces and hands at night as well as plucking their eyebrows and moustaches to form a finer line. But the most important features of masculine charm were the beards ; these were trimmed and cut into various forms long or short, pointed or spade shaped.

Gentlemen wore splendid doublets embroidered with an abundance of gold braid, lace, ribbons and jewels over padded 'bombasts' which curved outwards from the chest into a pot-bellied ridge down the front ending in a point below the tightly-laced waists. These bombasts were stuffed with horsehair, wool, flock or even bran ; an accidental tear in the cloth could result in a sudden deflation of the silhouette!

A short circular cloak, sometimes with sleeves, flared out from the shoulders. Breeches ballooned like giant pumpkins, slashed and puffed with padding. Both men and women wore knitted stockings of fine silk or wool, and shoes of similar styles made in leather, silk or velvet.

Scented gloves were worn by both sexes and pomanders hanging on chains from the ladies waists probably helped to keep away the less pleasant odours rising from the open sewers in the streets.

The inequality between rich and poor was marked by the difference in clothing. Instead of the silks and velvets worn by the merchant's wife, the poorer woman possessed one gown of rough wool, just as the squalor of rat infested hovels contrasted with the sumptuous furnishings, fine rugs and silver goblets of the wealthy.

1595

Kaüfer. Lorondes

1 2 3 4
5 6 7 8
9 10 11 12
13 14 15 16

On the next two pages you will find a costume model of 1595
Cut out the pages carefully along the cutting lines.
When making the model it is important to follow the assembly
order by numbers as shown above.

For general instructions on cutting, folding and glueing see
page 4.

On the back of the cutout pages there are patchwork patterns.
These form the patterned linings to the dresses, hats and ribbons etc.

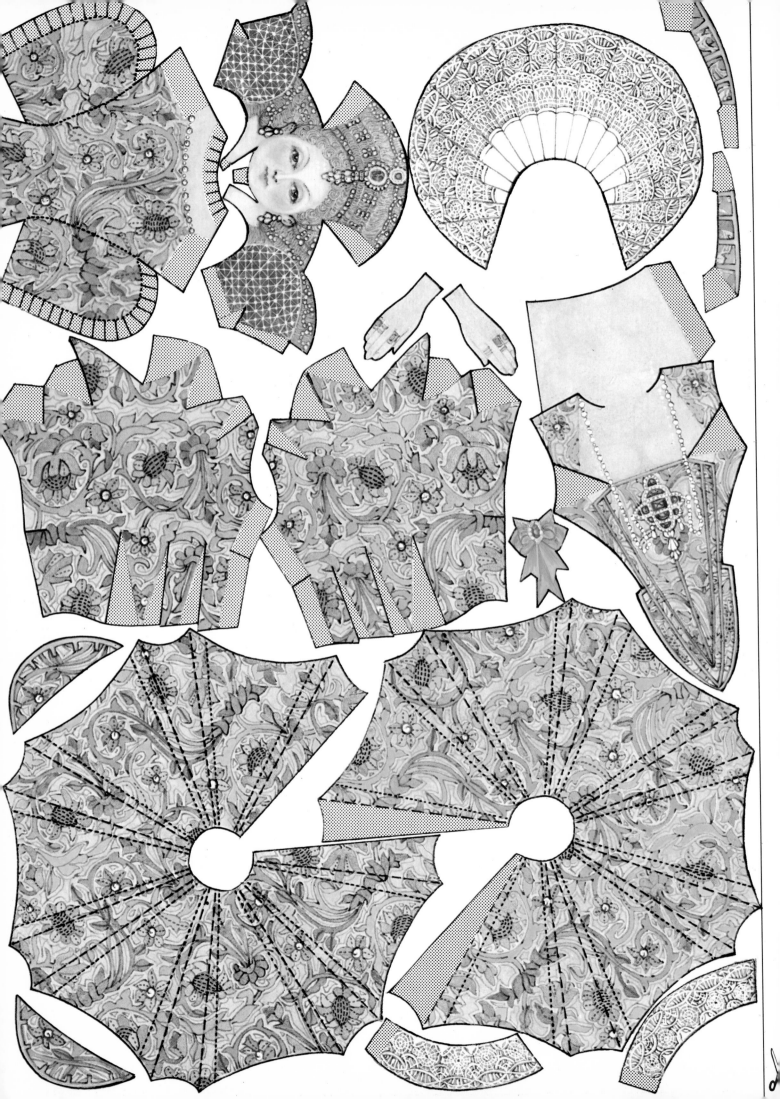

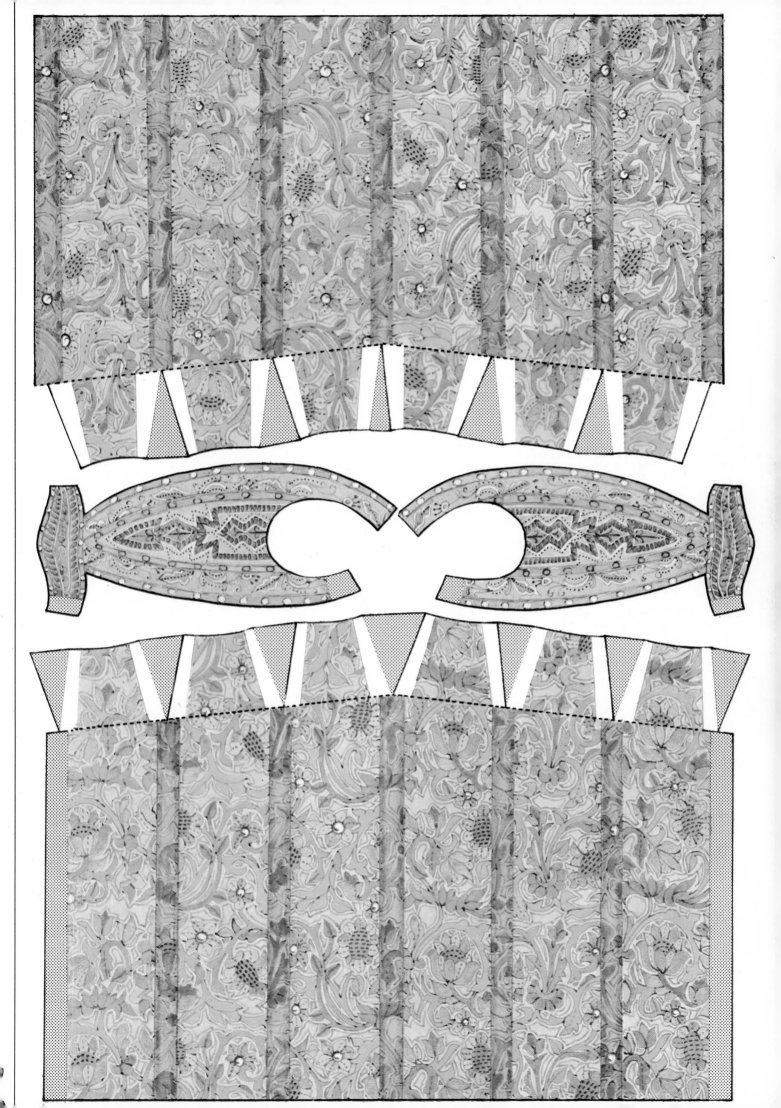

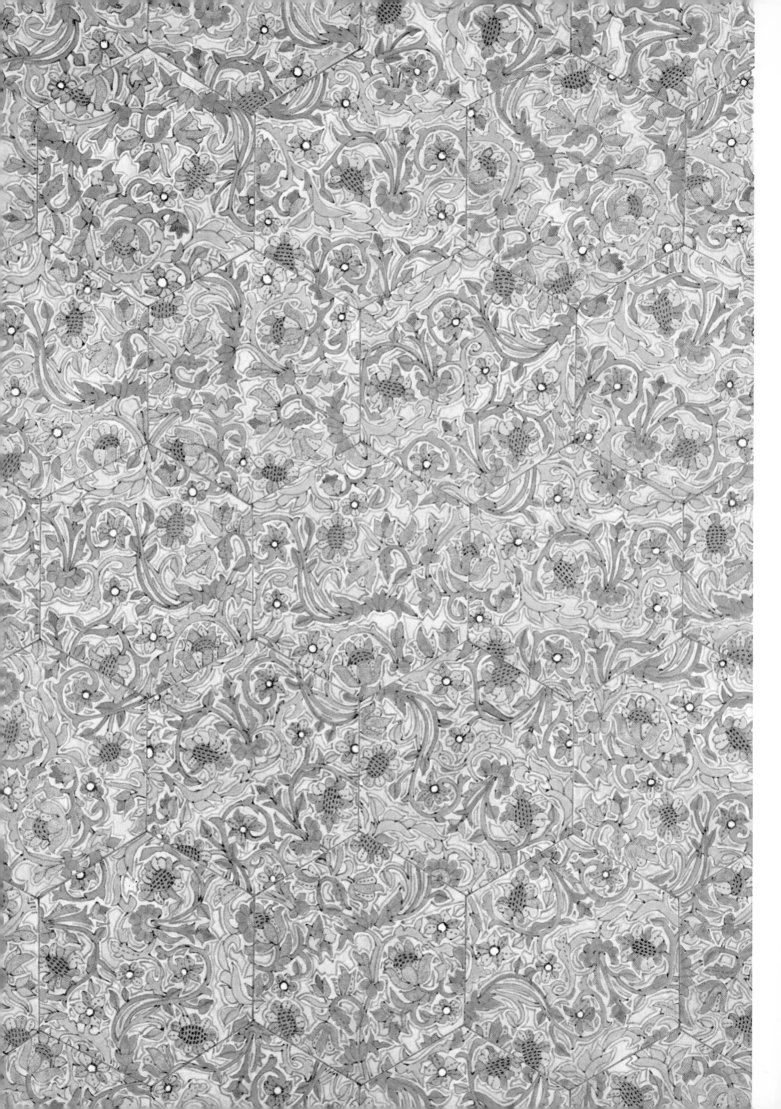

1615

1625

1630

1640

1640 PURITANS

3 In spite of the frequent periods of war and destruction throughout Europe, costume continued to develop in elegance and refinement, moving from formality towards a more relaxed look. During these times, styles of clothing were most strongly influenced by the French, and to a lesser extent, the Dutch.

Gradually ladies, no longer restricted by the severity of stiff corsets and excessive padding, gained not only comfort but a naturalness and simplicity of style. Instead of the farthingale, the long full-skirted gown hung free from the waist over slight padding, often pinned up in front or at the sides, to display a bright decorative petticoat or underskirt.

By 1640 waisted jackets were worn over the skirts, the jackets were laced down the chest over a small stomacher, and sashed under the breast with a silk ribbon belt tied with bows. Similar ribbons, bows and rosettes decorated the large puffed slashed 'virago' sleeves which ballooned out from the shoulder and were then caught in again at one or two places with jewelled clasps or ribbons. The hanging sleeve at the back had become smaller and shorter and now stopped at the elbow, the sleeves ended in turned-up lace cuffs, a little way above the wrists leaving the lower arm bare.

The starched ruff after having become gradually smaller disappeared to be replaced by a large collar made of layers of lace which fell gracefully over the shoulders and around the deep neckline of the low-cut dress.

Stiff brocades were no longer admired; instead soft draperies of satin, velvet and silks were skilfully and subtly blended in contrasting colours and materials, trimmed with a variety of ribbons and lace. The rich luxury of gleaming coloured silks caught the light in the gathered folds of materials expressing the flamboyant and romantic spirit of the time.

Ladies wore their hair shoulder-length brushed flat on top, with a small fringe and frizzed out at the sides often gathered into a cluster of ringlets and prettily tied together with charming bows or strings of pearls. It was now fashionable to have dark hair, so fair young ladies coloured their hair with brown powder. It was the custom to do away with a head-covering indoors, but out of doors ladies would protect their fair complexions with broad brimmed felt or beaver-skin hats topped with flowing ostrich plumes, like those of the men, and worn at a jaunty angle. Ladies venturing out of the house often wore masks to protect their faces from the weather, or to conceal their identity. Make-up was heavy, and consisted of powdered white lead, flour, rice, quicksilver or bismuth, patches were stuck to the face and seductively placed on the bosom.

Women's shoes were beautifully embroidered and expensive, so specially constructed wooden soles fastened over the shoes with leather straps called 'pattens' or 'chopines', were worn to protect the elegant footwear from the mud in the streets. At times the soles were so high that they lifted the wearer many inches off the ground.

To keep their hands warm in the winter, both men and women carried large muffs made of velvet, satin or fur. Men, too, adopted the custom of sticking on small face patches cut out of black silk or taffeta in the forms of stars or crescents or various other shapes. The dashing worldliness of the men of these times has seldom been equalled. With their rich lace and bright sashes, their short cloaks nonchalantly tossed over a shoulder to show off the contrasting coloured lining, young men of good birth were less restricted than women in the display of lace and linen on the cuffs and wide falling collars, over their velvet or satin suits.

Men now wore a form of unpadded doublet which was not buttoned right up to the neck and fell open below the waist to show off the shirt, usually made of fine white linen or silk. Doublet sleeves were slashed to show the full shirt beneath and the tightly fastened wrists were trimmed with deep turned back cuffs of lace.

In time longer breeches replaced the short trunk hose and lost their padding, gradually developing away from the previous baggy and loose shape, and narrowing from the waist to be fastened just below the knee by rosettes or bows of ribbon.

The materials used for doublets and breeches although rich, were plain and unadorned and colours were paler with contrasting trimmings.

With the breeches, bucket top boots of soft wrinkled leather were worn, either pushed down so that they hung loose and flopping below the knee, or else pulled up to the thigh for riding. Stockings or boot-hose were trimmed with a deep lace flounce which frothed over the tops of the boots. As well as boots, shoes of leather with thick high heels, squared toes and elaborate buckles, often decorated with huge rosettes, were worn; scarlet heels being popular with full dress or Court wear. With the shoes, silk stockings were gartered at the top with fancy ribbons and rosettes and to enhance the shape of the leg, men's stockings were sometimes padded to make up for nature's deficiency.

Although tradesmen and workers wore their hair 'bobbed' or of medium length the man of fashion, having discarded the stiff starched ruff, now wore his hair in shoulder length flowing locks and sometimes when courting a lady he attached a ribbon bow to a curl. Beards were trimmed to a fashionable point and the upturned moustache was curled with hot curling tongs.

In addition to the profusion of lace and ribbons, jewelled brooches and buttons adorned both men and women. Although men favoured a single ear ring, pearl drop ear rings were fashionable for women throughout this period. Sword hilts were also elaborately made of precious metals and decorated with jewels.

The distinction in dress which separated the nobility from the mass of the people was as great as ever. However, the merchant, with his new found wealth, began to copy the aristocracy, which forced the nobles to change styles constantly in order to maintain a difference of social class that was immediately obvious in their clothing.

Whilst the dashing cavalier and his lady dressed in a dazzling array of colours, lace and ribbons, some of the British puritans and the Dutch Protestants went to equal extremes of severe simplicity, wearing dark colours such as black, greys and browns, and proving their religious beliefs by the quiet modesty and humility of their dress.

1640

1 2 3 4
5 6 7 8
9 10 11 12
13 14 15 16
17

On the next two pages you will find a costume model of 1640
Cut out the pages carefully along the cutting lines.
When making the model it is important to follow the assembly
order by numbers as shown above.

For general instructions on cutting, folding and glueing see
page 4.

On the back of the cutout pages there are patchwork patterns.
These form the patterned linings to the dresses, hats and ribbons etc.

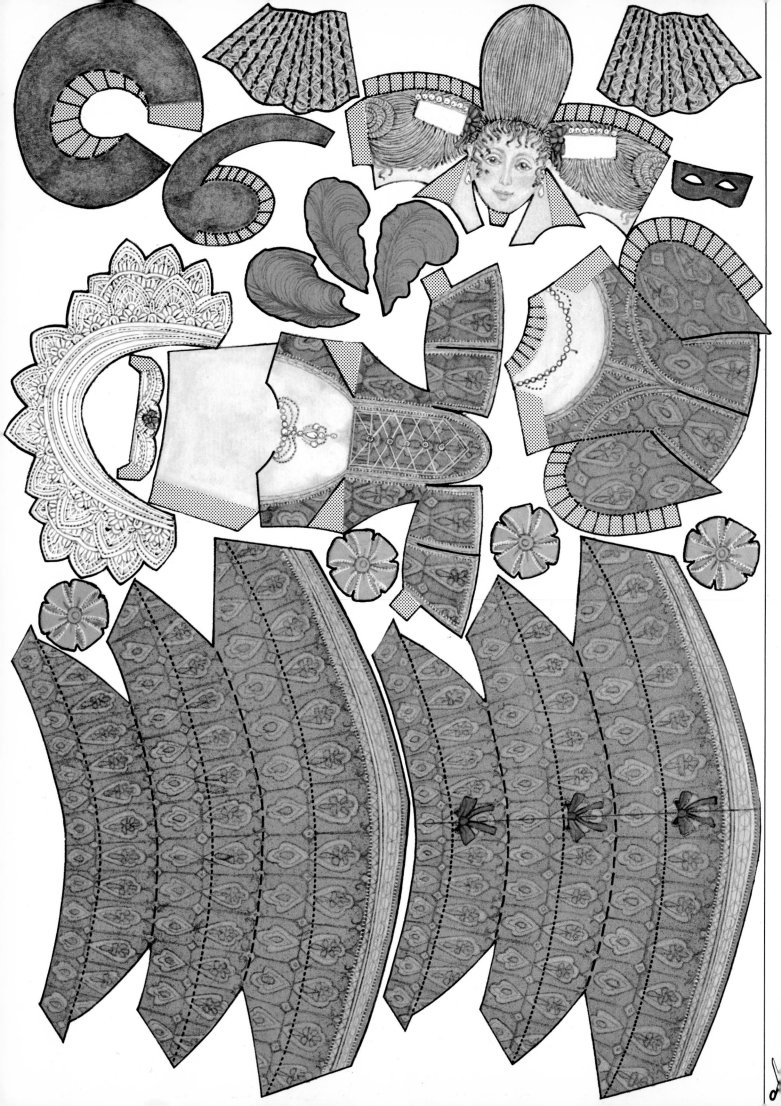

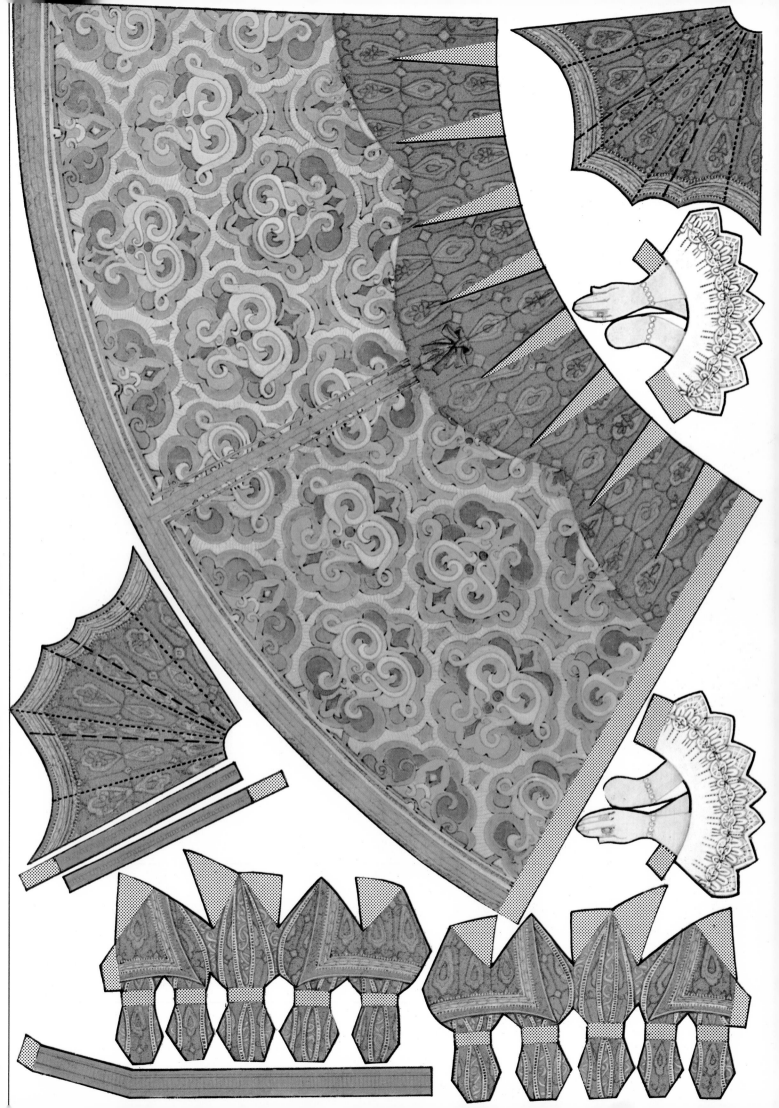

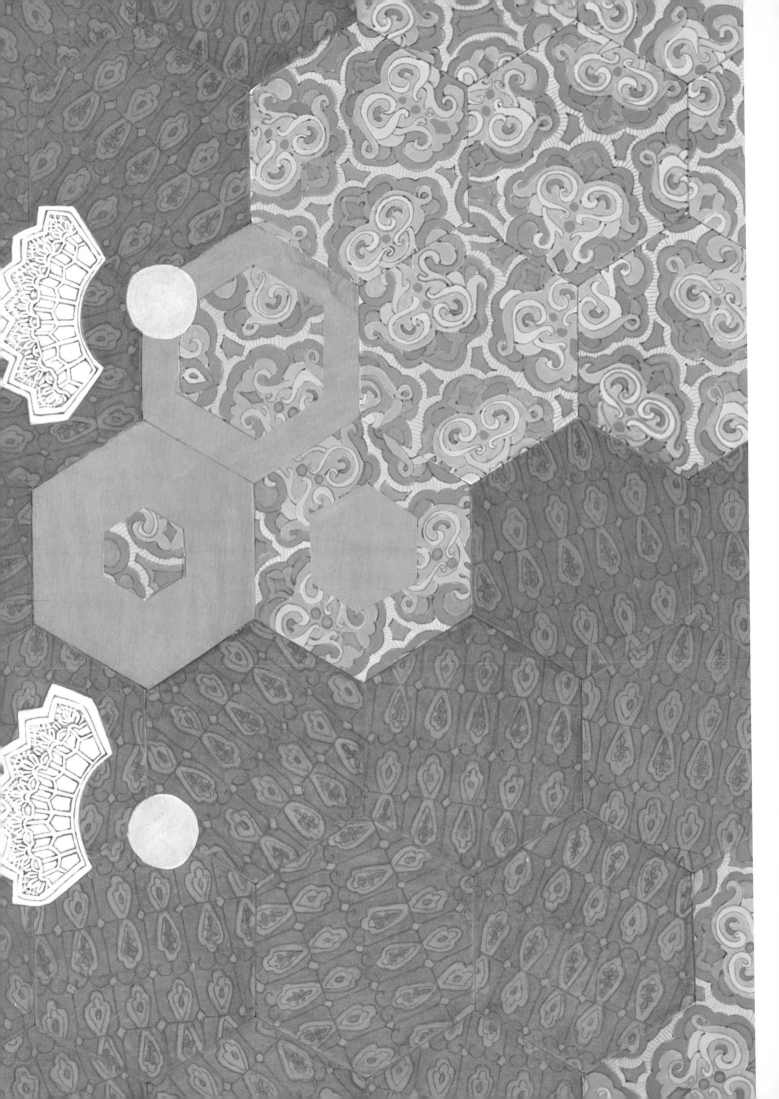

1646 **1660** **1670** **1695** **1730** **1740** **1756**

4 Fashions continued for a while in the lavish styles of the 1640s. Then jackets and virago sleeves disappeared and dresses with low collars were opened in the front to show beautiful elaborate underskirts. Gentlemen wore wide baggy trousers, with shorter jackets allowing the shirts to be pulled out at the waist.

In the 1690s the grandiose splendour of Louis XIV's Court at Versailles, developed a new, stiff elegance of costume to match the architecture. For the ladies the open skirt was now pulled back and piled up at the rear on a support, exposing petticoats made of heavily embroidered brocades, opulently tasselled and fringed in gold cords and braids. The bodice was cut low and square and the stomacher accentuated the tiny corseted waist, as the sleeves grew tighter, ending in ruffles below the elbow. The hair was decorated by a high wired 'Fontange' cap of pleated lace.

Gentlemen wore knee-breeches under tight-waisted coats which were stiffened below the waist to flare out into wide long pleated skirts. Gold braids outlined the shape of the coat with the huge turned back cuffs and low pockets. Wigs gradually became larger, with a centre parting ending in trailing masses of curls and ringlets.

The stuffy formality of these clothes gave way eventually to a new delicacy and lightness. By the early 1700s a new gaiety and easy grace was displayed in the interior decoration; as mirrors, furniture and panellings were carved and moulded into twisted fanciful shell-like shapes. A new softness and prettiness was introduced into women's clothes in France as they ceased to be made by tailors and instead were cut and styled by ladies dressmakers.

After 1730 the shape of ladies' skirts changed from a circle to an oval as the front and back of the skirt was flattened and the sides spread out extending to as wide as 180 centimetres (two yards) either side of the hips. This was supported by wide hoops at the sides called 'Panniers' (from the French word for baskets). To pass through doorways the wide

hipped women had to sidle sideways, until this was eventually overcome by the invention of hinged panniers which could be folded up and held under the arms.

Necklines became square and low, with a series of graduated pretty ribbon bows forming ladders (échelles) which ran down the front of the stomacher, to the waist. the skirt generally opened in the front and was bordered with ruffles or flowers and lace over a decorative flounced underskirt. Long vertical box pleats were stitched at the top of the back of the shoulders, hanging loose behind and falling in elegant folds to the ground, with a short train. The dresses cut tightly to fit the corsetted waist, were made of light, fine Indian silks and muslins, in fresh clean colours and pale tones of white, rose-pinks, cream, or soft apple greens, edged in ruffled bands of silk with flower motifs—materials which were ideal for this enchantingly delicate fashion. The short, tight, elbow-length sleeves ending in more ruffles and the diminutive waist, combined with the little light running steps, as though they were gliding across the floor on wheels, all stressed the effect of the fragile, frivolous woman.

Hair was drawn back, swept up into a small bun or plait and powdered white with wheatmeal or rice meal. Special closets or cabinets were reserved for this procedure, the woman hiding her face in a bag as the scented powder was sprayed up into the air to fall evenly over her head.

In the early 18th century hats were hardly ever worn, later the swept up hairstyle was enhanced by flattering small hats, with upturned brims often three-cornered (tricorne), in shape. The simple country style, adopted from England, led to the wearing of wide brimmed, rustic straw hats trimmed and tied with ribbons, over a small close-fitting milkmaid mob-cap of white muslin.

Ladies' shoes had pointed toes and were made in silk, satin, brocade or kid decorated with valuable jewelled metal buckles, with very tall heels, often red.

At this time there was a certain restraint in the wearing of jewellery; however with beautiful buttons, elbow length gloves, small handsome muffs and fans and maybe, a little black boy to carry the long handled painted silk parasol over the lady of fashion, there seemed little need for other accessories.

This was an age of interest in the arts, and ladies of high society presided over salons (drawing rooms), entertaining the famous writers, painters, politicians, and philosophers. Fashion now followed high society rather than imitating noble courtiers.

This was also reflected in the dress of the men in their clean-cut, fitted costumes. Their tight-waisted narrow-shouldered coats ended just above the knee, the coat skirts were re-inforced with canvas and horsehair so that they stood out from the hips. Coats were made of rich satins, silks, plush, velvets and brocades, with elaborate embroidery on the large pocket flaps and buttoned cuffs. The waistcoat was a veritable work of art in rich embroidery, stiffened with buckram or coarse linen to spring out from the hips in front of the coat. The neck cravat made of linen or muslin, was loosely knotted and tucked into the frilled shirt, whose ruffled shirt sleeves protruded from under the coat cuffs.

The knee-breeches were made with a full seat which was tightened by buckles at the back; the legs of these breeches were buttoned just below the knees.

Men's shoes became more rounded at the toe, with bold buckles; the tonges and the heels now smaller than before, and red heels were still fashionable for dress wear. Stockings were ribbed or chequered, and were made of different colours.

Men wore wigs in a variety of styles. They were usually powdered, and the lock of hair behind was caught back and tied in a ribbon low on the neck. Because of the powdered wigs, the three-cornered hat, its brim bound with braid, was more often than not carried under the arm rather than worn.

The man about town took as much trouble as the ladies over his make-up; he reddened his lips, decorated his cheeks with patches, scented his linen, carefully dressed his wig and plucked his eyebrows. He carried a lace handkerchief as an accessory, which he casually held between his fingers. It was said at the time that "a slovenly fellow might hustle into his clothes in an hour but a gentleman could scarcely dress in less than two!"

1750

1

2

3

4

5

6

7

8

9

10

11

12

13

14

15

16

17

On the next two pages you will find a costume model of 1750
Cut out the pages carefully along the cutting lines.
When making the model it is important to follow the assembly
order by numbers as shown above.

For general instructions on cutting, folding and glueing see
page 4.

On the back of the cutout pages there are patchwork patterns.
These form the patterned linings to the dresses, hats and ribbons etc.

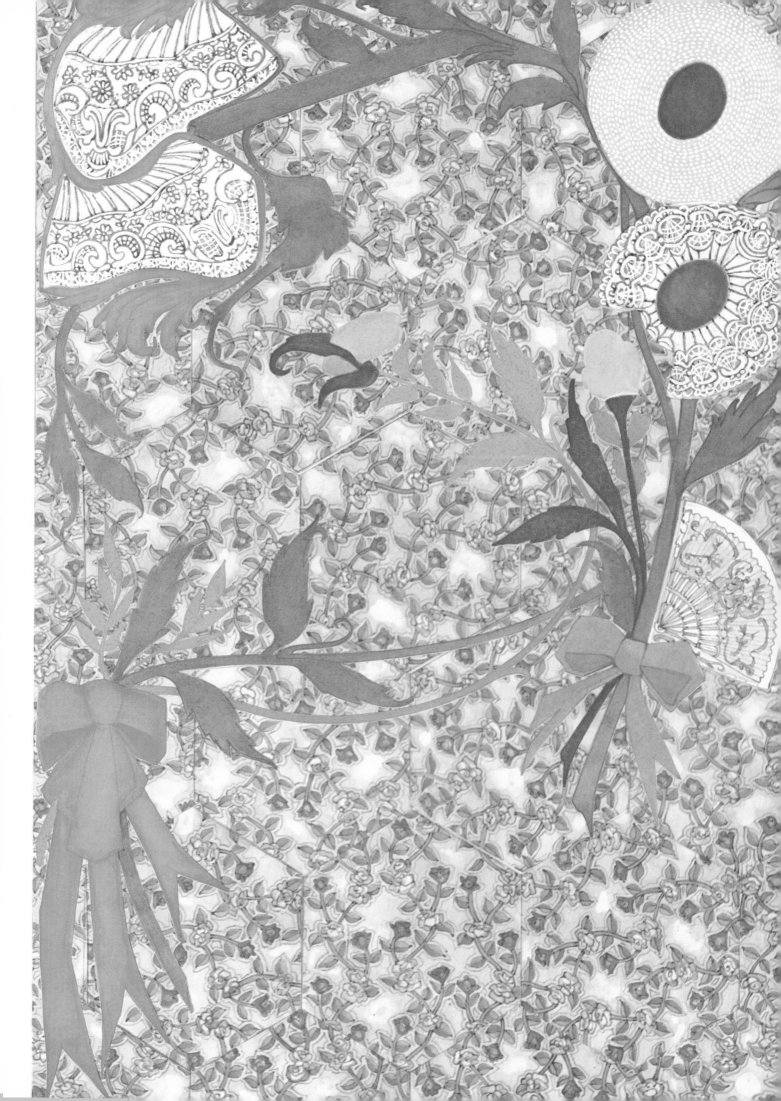

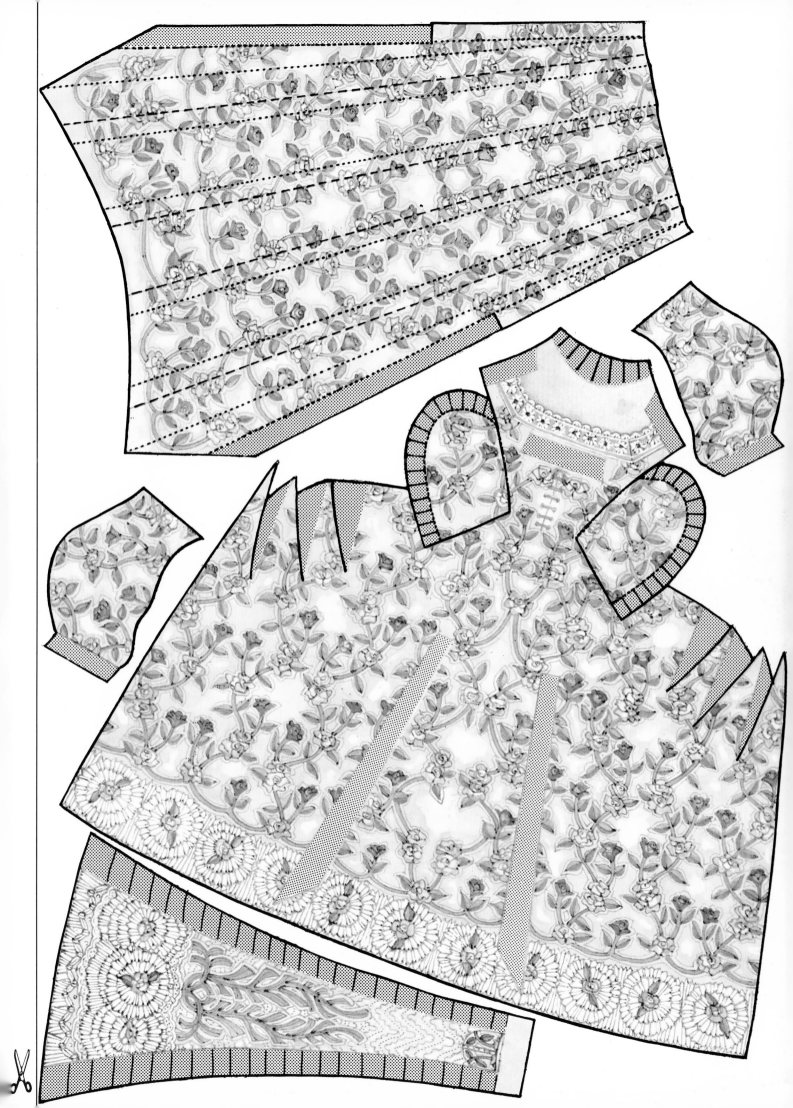

1765

1770

1772

1775

1780

5   The rise of industry in the eighteenth century brought new wealth created by the invention of many new machines. The grand life of the rich and powerful contrasted strongly to the hardship, poverty, and squalor suffered by the labouring classes. However, amongst many far-thinking people, it was a time of growing awareness of social injustices. The revolutionary war in America which won Americans complete independence from England was later to encourage the poor people of France to rise up against the indifference of their rulers. France not only sent naval and military aid to America but French fashions, too, were readily accepted by wealthy colonists, for France was still the leader in matters of style. Fashionable women eagerly awaited the arrival of the carefully constructed boxes containing detailed fashion dolls, beautifully formed in paper, showing the latest Paris styles. Towards the end of the eighteenth century, hand painted, engraved fashion plates replaced the dolls, and dressmakers could use these engravings to discuss dresses with their customers.

The Queen of France, Marie Antoinette, was indeed the Queen of fashion. Completely out of touch with reality, the Queen and ladies of her Court enjoyed their extravagant tastes, adapting and romantisicing their own frivolous version of the dresses of milkmaids and shepherdesses, as they amused themselves with a farm built specially for them in the grounds of the Palace of Versailles. There is little doubt that the costly whims of the Queen and her Court helped to build up the smouldering resentment that led to the raging fire of the French Revolution and her eventual execution at the guillotine.

Panniers and hoops were only worn at court, otherwise they vanished and were replaced by an existing fashion, which was altered and adapted for everyday wear, called the Polonaise.

Most dresses were made with an opening in the side seams, so that women could reach into the special side pockets which were tied by tapes around the waist beneath the petticoat. As the petticoat was slightly shorter than the dress, the more active ladies gathered up the two bottom corners of the over-gown and pushed them through the opening in the side seams, looping up the skirts as they did so to give the effect of festoons of material. This fashion continued, until by 1780 the skirts were draped by cords or tapes pulled through rings sewn inside the dress, to hold the folds more firmly and permanently in place. The low neckline of the Polonaise was tied at the bosom with a large bow. A small scarf or kerchief lay around the shoulders, folded over with the ends tucked into the neckline. Dresses were made of satin, silk, printed cotton, or muslin in plain or striped materials. The waistline was natural and a small bustle or false rump was worn to give padding to the skirt.

The extravagance of the French fashion was nowhere better to be seen than in the women's hairdressing, where the grotesque elaborate fantasies of false plaits and tresses were supported on pads and piled up and raised to absurd and exaggerated heights of over 90 centimetres (three feet). These creations were smeared with scented ointment and then heavily powdered. Into the hair were fastened pins, ribbons, feathers and various ornaments, such as artificial birds, cardboard cupids, bunches of vegetables, models of coaches, windmills, and even ships in full sail. These monstrous structures became so cumbersome that women had to sit on the floor when riding in coaches. Once built, the heavily powdered construction remained in place for days or even weeks, providing a warm comfortable hiding place for fleas so that a long-handled scratching-stick was a practical accessory!

To protect these large wigs out of doors, a large collapsible 'calash' hood, made like a pram hood, of hoops and whalebone, padded and covered in silk, could be opened up or closed down over the hair by means of cords. Less ostentatious ladies wore simpler, smaller wigs or dusted over their own hair with grey powder, this was then dressed with ringlets framing the face, hanging at times to touch the shoulders. Often perched on top of the head and held there with pins was a straw tricorne or turban hat trimmed with gauze or feathers. Ladies' shoes were made of silk or brocades decorated with jewels and buckles, with high curved heels.

Men's clothes in France still consisted of close-fitting, embroidered dress coats in satin or velvet, cut away in front to narrow coat-tails ending at the back of the knees. The double-breasted coats were generally buttoned up so that only the bottom of the waistcoat was seen. The collar was high, turned down and faced with velvet. The embroidered waistcoat was shorter than before and cut-away ending in two v-shaped points. Tight breeches in black velvet or satin extended just below the knee and were buckled or fastened by ribbons.

Men's wigs became smaller and more discreet and were worn in many styles, but towards the end of the century two or three horizontal rolls of hair were placed at the sides, and the whole crown of the hair was swept back without a parting. Beneath the wig the natural hair was cut short, and at night the wig would rest beside the bed on a wig stand. The most popular hat was the tricorne which was almost always black, edged with fringing or gold braid. Shoes were flat-soled and made of black leather, with shining silver buckles. A silver knobbed cane and a quizzing glass suspended from a black ribbon helped to complete the wardrobe of the French gentleman.

A fresh wind of change was blowing over from England, as the English simplicity of style now began to influence some of the French ideas of dress. The English noblemen, unlike their French equivalents, generally disliked Court life and preferred the freedom of their large estates. When they came to town on business or pleasure, they wore the same casual clothing made of woollen cloth in practical colours, that were designed for riding and shooting. The English lady borrowed and adapted the sporting masculine styles of the English men wearing long riding coats with shoulder capes, large lapels, bold buttons triple collars, and pocket flaps, over her dresses, as well as sensible skirts and jackets.

These English fashions rapidly gained in popularity in France, where the over-dressed French nobleman promenading with his lady was about to witness the French Revolution, and the disintegration of the world as they knew it.

1780

1 2 3 4
5 6 7 8
9 10 11 12
13 14 15

On the next two pages you will find a costume model of 1780
Cut out the pages carefully along the cutting lines.
When making the model it is important to follow the assembly
order by numbers as shown above.

For general instructions on cutting, folding and glueing see
page 4.

On the back of the cutout pages there are patchwork patterns.
These form the patterned linings to the dresses, hats and ribbons etc.

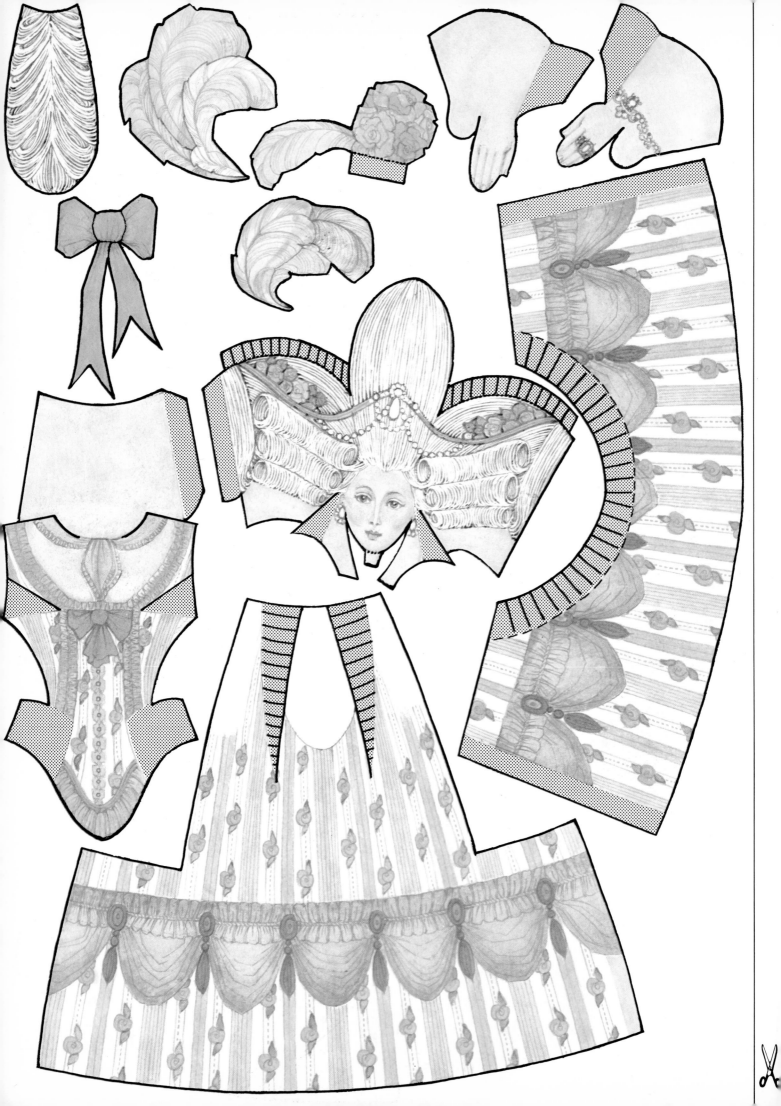

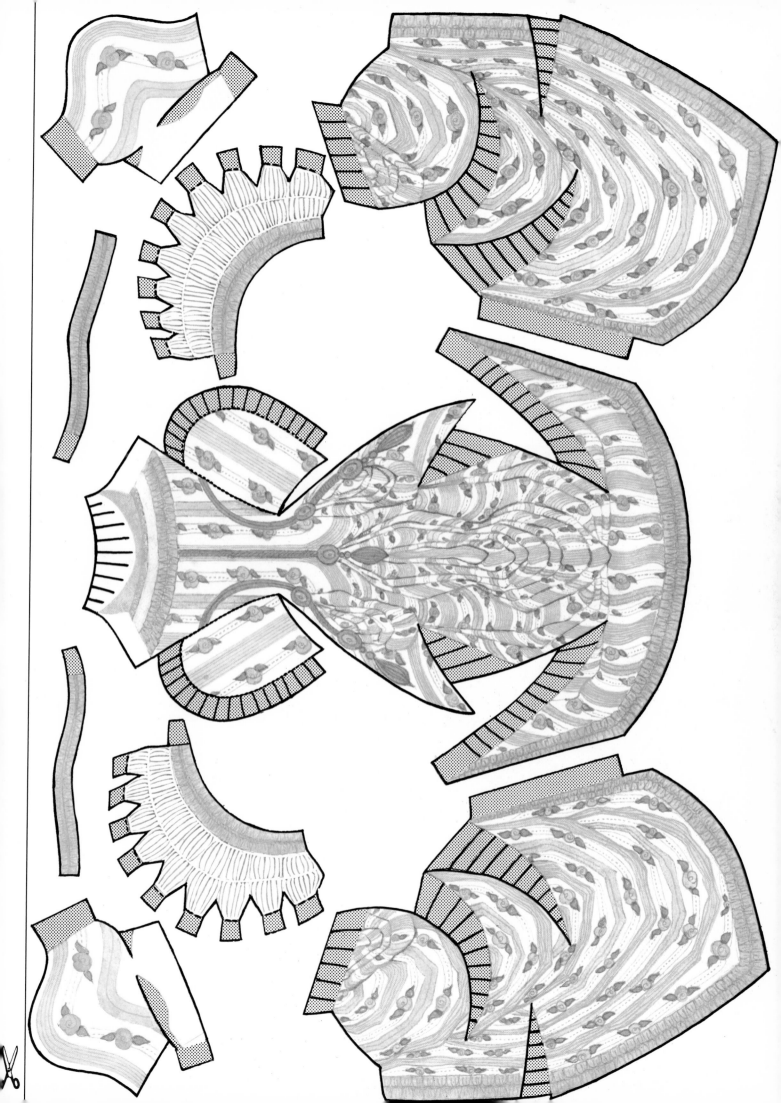

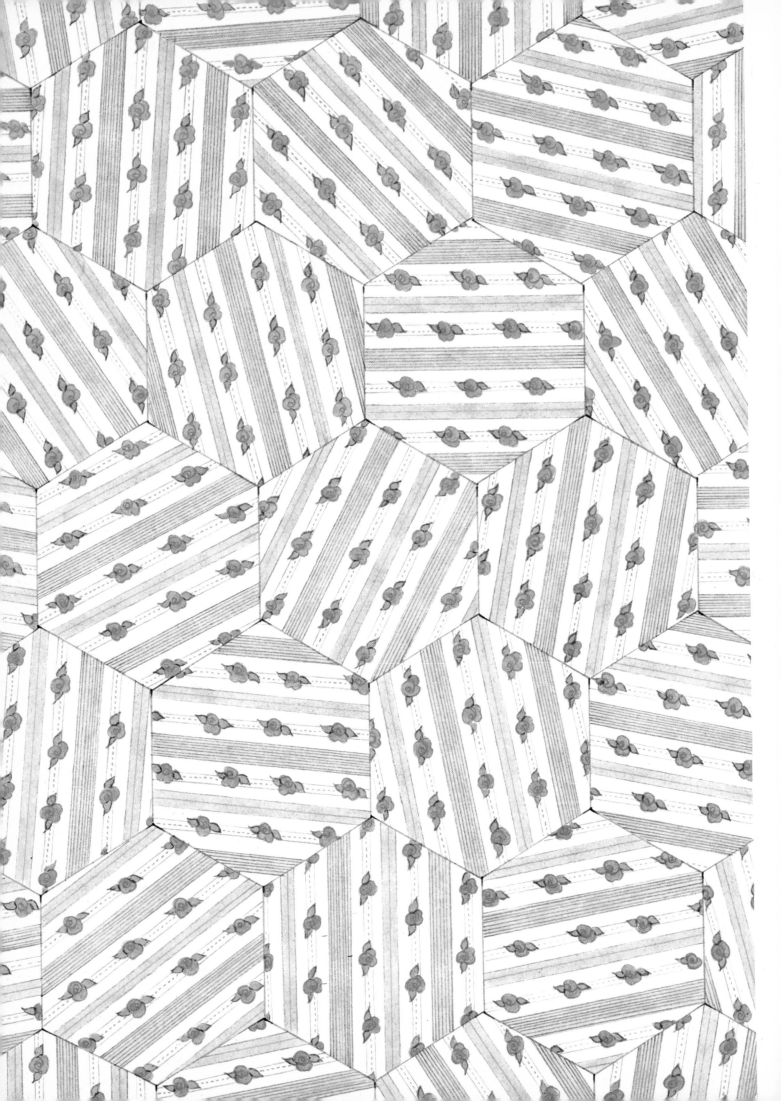

1780

1790

1795

1796

1802

1815

6 The English country styles continued in popularity throughout Europe and gentlemen's clothes were more sober and well cut. As ladies hairdressing became simpler, their hats grew larger and more flamboyant. Gentle muslin dresses were worn with a natural waistline and a soft fichu (scarf) puffed out and draped around the neck to look pigeon-chested, Then came the French Revolution and a dramatic change in fashion.

No one could survive the reign of Terror during the French Revolution if they continued the customs and flaunted the clothes of the Royalists. To escape attention and avoid denunciation and the danger of death at the guillotine it was necessary to dress as one of the people. Therefore fashion meant a display of simplicity, liberty and equality in costume. When the threat of the guillotine had passed, there was an upsurge of freedom of expression that was immediately reflected in the fashions worn by the carefree and spirited youth. They dressed in outrageous clothes ; the young men called 'incroyables' (incredibles), wore high collars with enormous cravats that covered not only the neck, but the chin as well, and generally carried their clothing to extremes of ridiculous exaggeration. The young women 'merveilleuses' (the marvellous ones), admired the classic Greek and Roman dress, which they adapted into high waisted and transparent dresses, daringly slit from waist to hem, worn with open Roman sandals on their feet and rings on their toes. Hair of both sexes was wild, short, straggly and totally dishevelled.

Revolutionary France was caught up in wars with neighbouring nations. In the beginning, victories in Italy, Spain and Portugal brought General Bonaparte power and fame. In 1804 Napoleon, at the age of thirty, became Emperor of the French.

The dream of Napoleon was a romantic vision of the Roman empire, so the flowing classical lines of ancient Roman

clothes were transformed into fragile white muslin and the delicate textures of net, gauze and lace. The dresses were semi-transparent sheaths with the necklines low-cut and square exposing most of the bosom, and the arms were bare. Immediately below the breasts, the high waists were encircled with a narrow belt, allowing the skirt to fall in graceful, soft folds to the feet. Underneath the dress was worn a flesh coloured body stocking which gave a daring impression of nudity. It was not long before Napoleon decided that the dignity of the state was in question, which brought in a new sense of modesty to Frenchwomen, and through them to the rest of Europe and America. The bare arms were covered in long coloured gloves to be replaced gradually by long narrow sleeves with small puffs on the shoulders. The bare bosom was filled in with gauze and ended in a ruffled collarette around the neck. The smartest fashion accessory was the brightly coloured shawl, the more expensive ones came from Kashmir in India, but cheaper imitations were made and found an instant market. There was an art to wearing the shawl, it could be draped behind the back and over the arms, or else trailed along the floor.

The simple sheath dress was now no longer semi-transparent. Made of heavier silks it was embroidered with floral decorative motifs; the hem of the skirt was padded and swags of ruched ribbons or fabrics were added to give greater richness and weight.

Since the light weight gowns gave no protection from the cold winter, even though stiffened petticoats and knee drawers were worn underneath, an outer garment was introduced in the form of a fur-lined coat with a hood. This was the origin of the coat as we know it today.

The Napoleonic wars influenced women's dress in Europe; froggings, epaulettes and braid—the trimmings of military uniforms—became part of the fashion-conscious ladies' wardrobe. At first women's hair was cut short—a fashionable reminder of preparations for the guillotine. Later it was arranged in the soft flattering forms of the ancient Greek style. This led to the wearing of all types of bonnets and turbans fitting closely to the head, the most popular hat was the tall-crowned French bonnet decorated with sprays of artificial flowers, tied under the chin with bright ribbons with the wide brim sweetly framing the face. To achieve a pale, fragile, interesting look, white face powder was used, without rouge.

For walking front-laced boots of soft kid were comfortable and for evening wear and dancing white satin slippers were fashionable and pretty. Both had small, very low heels or no heels at all, and white silk stockings showed off a delightful trim ankle.

It was necessary to carry small fabric bags, for dresses allowed no place for pockets. Fans were small and discreet and jewellery was worn sparingly.

From the French Revolution onwards the centre of fashion for the man passed from Paris to London. The informality and independence of the English gentleman with his dislike of fussy detail in his casual country wear, was carried to the ultimate elegance in the carefully fitted and perfectly tailored suits encouraged by the Prince Regent, and his dandy friends such as Beau Brummel.

Ornate silk embroidery disappeared from men's clothes to be replaced by a new crisp concept of scrupulous cleanliness.

The double breasted tail coat was cut square and then sloped away from the waist leaving the thighs free. The coats were of plain colours usually in dark blue, black, olive green or plum. Beneath the waistcoat was worn a linen shirt with a muslin frill at the neck or else high starched white collars with the points reaching the cheeks, tied by a broad tightly-wrapped cravat, the meticulous knotting of which was the most important part of a man's dress.

The tight, light-coloured breeches were fastened by small buttons on the outside of the legs below the knees and were tucked into highly polished black leather riding boots with tan-coloured tops.

During the daytime out of doors, single breasted greatcoats trimmed with fur collars and cuffs were worn, for evening wear the greatcoats were exchanged for cloaks. Hairstyles for men were classical, cut fairly short and brushed forward onto the face without a parting, in soft curls or strands. All gentlemen wore hats of silk or beaver, with curled up brims; the crowns were large but of moderate height, in colours of black, fawn or grey. Men's jewellery was inconspicuous, consisting merely of a gold watch, fob and chain.

For the first time in the history of fashion it was now stylish to be discreet.

1815

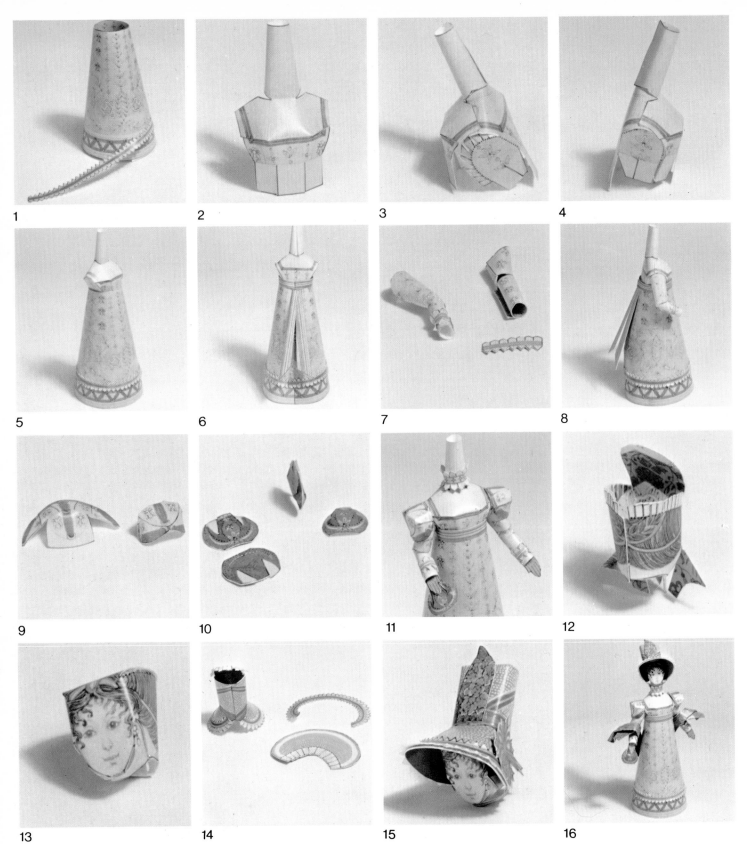

1   2   3   4

5   6   7   8

9   10   11   12

13   14   15   16

On the next two pages you will find a costume model of 1815
Cut out the pages carefully along the cutting lines.
When making the model it is important to follow the assembly
order by numbers as shown above.

For general instructions on cutting, folding and glueing see
page 4.

On the back of the cutout pages there are patchwork patterns.
These form the patterned linings to the dresses, hats and ribbons etc.

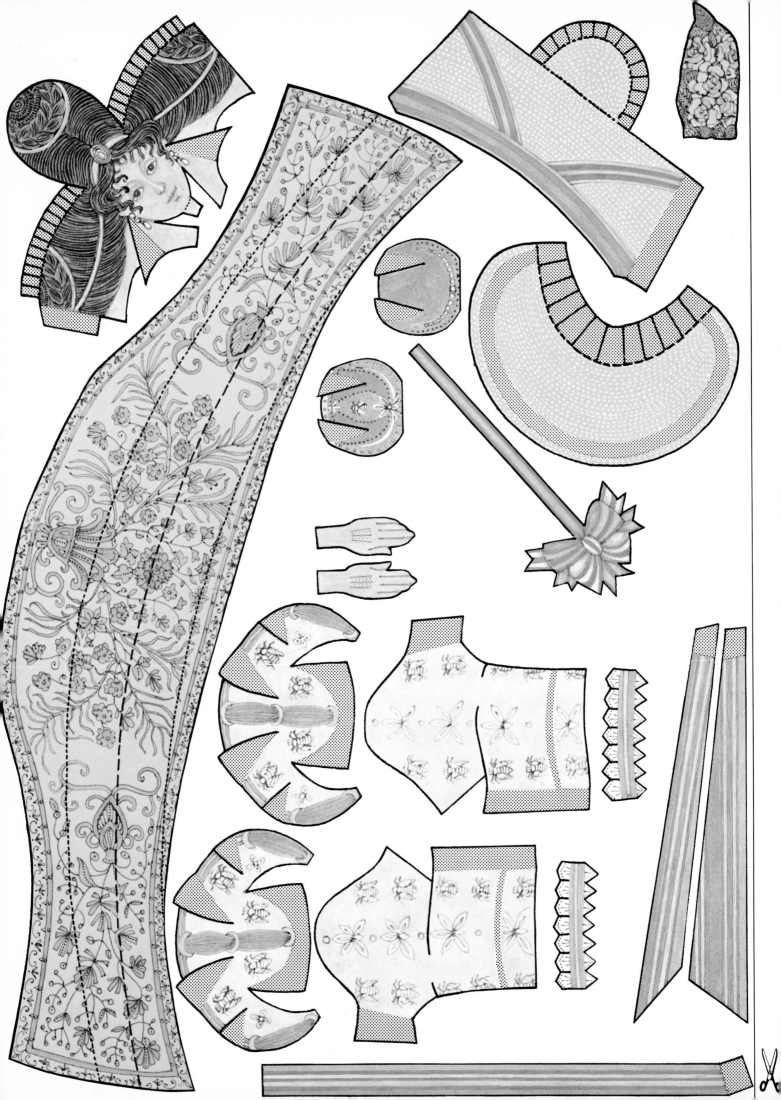

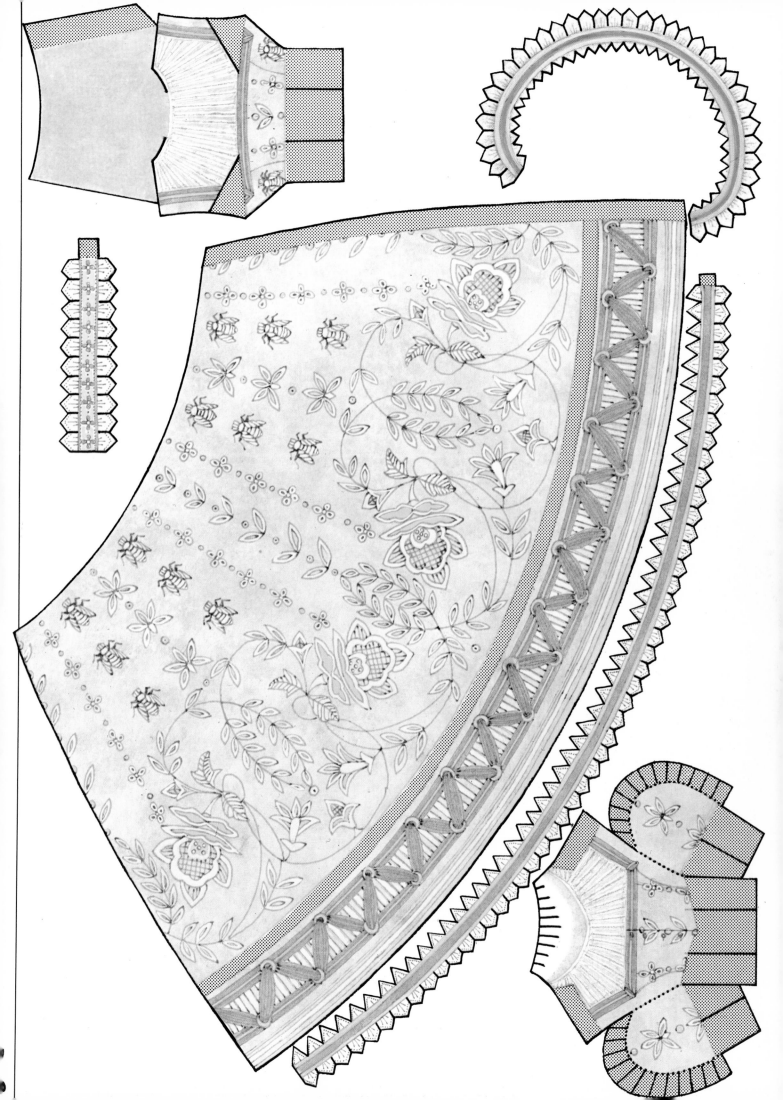

1825

1835

1850

1860

7 In Paris in the 1820s the Empire waistline dropped to its natural position immediately above the hips. Tightly laced corsets squeezed and compressed the waist into the now fashionable hour-glass figure. Sleeves were puffed out, giving a top heavy downward sloping appearance at the shoulder line whilst the skirt was widened at the hem with padded bands and decorations. This was topped by wide hats and bonnets decorated with streaming ribbons and fluttering feathers.

Following similar lines as the women, the fashionable men of this period wore an ample loose frock coat thrown open to display deep rolling padded collars and wide lapels, emphasising the narrow waist and retaining a military swagger and self-confidence showed in the variety of colours used for waistcoats, gloves, and cravats. This was virtually the last splash of colour to be seen in men's dress.

After 1830 trousers were well and truly established. First introduced in the early 1800s, they were at first skin-tight and ended above the ankle, then fell loosely to the feet fastened under the shoes by means of straps. In contrast to the dark coats in sombre hues of blue or brown, trousers were light grey or fawn. For town wear a symbol of respectability was the tall shiny cylindrical top hat with a large brim later reducing in width.

Every year the spread of the ladies' skirt made a wider circle, supported by up to seven petticoats made of starched muslin, flannel, padded cotton or quilted down, these became so heavy that walking was difficult.

Fashion was undergoing one of those strange changes for which it is famous. From the simple comfortable sheath-like dress of the Empire period, the almost incredible crinoline arrived on the scene. To support the volume of these large gowns which covered the women's long lace trimmed pantaloons, at first pads of horse hair (crin in French) were

introduced to make their skirts stand out. Later a stiff dome-shaped crinoline cage was introduced, consisting of an ever increasing circumference towards the hem, of bamboo, whalebone or steel hoops suspended on tapes; its lightness gave a much greater freedom of movement.

The crinoline stayed in fashion for over twenty years during which time even the charming habit of a gentleman giving his arm to a lady had to be abandoned, and to sit beside a woman on a sofa was impossible, as women were made unapproachable by their skirts. You could hold their hands but not embrace them.

This was a time when a desire to dwell on the tragedies of life was reflected in the cultivated delicate appearance, to look pale and faint into a trance was considered to be delightfully feminine. But with the increase in width of the dress women seemed to develop a self-confidence in society and the fragile angel of the 1800s was transformed into the heavily draped matronly woman of the 1860s.

From 1860 crinoline cages were flattened in front, and the fullness was concentrated at the back, extending in length almost into a train. The day dress was usually high-necked and the tiny waist was squeezed into a boned and laced corset. Large decorated 'pagoda' sleeves were worn over under-sleeves of white tulle or puffed muslin which were gathered in at the wrist and enriched with rows of lace. Large heavily fringed and braided shawls or capes were draped over the huge sleeves and voluminous skirts during the winter months. Pastel shades and white were popular for evening wear. Evening gowns were in silks and other light materials, with deeply cut necklines to expose the shoulders.

Deep purple, magenta, dark green and brown materials were fashionable during the daytime; the dresses heavily decorated with stripes and bands in contrasting colours, of silk, velvet or plush edged with rows of tassels and fringes.

The impracticability of the crinolines led to the short-lived introduction of loose baggy trousers gathered in at the ankles, by the courageous American Mrs. Amelia Bloomer, who at least if not able to establish a new fashion gave her name to womens knickers until more recent times.

The hair was brushed down smoothly from a centre parting, kept simple in style, with a low bun circular plaits over the ears, or side curls falling onto the cheeks.

At first the brim of the poke bonnets rose high from the forehead but after 1840 it shrank in size, no longer hiding the face but worn well back on the head, with ruchings and long tabs tied under the chin. Bonnets were made in velvet and silk or light straw and were often trimmed inside or out with feathers or bows of fine ribbons.

Outdoor shoes were long and narrow with square toes and high shaped heels. Boots of white satin, kid or coloured silks were also worn to just above the ankle, either laced or buttoned up or with elastic at the inner side, usually with white stockings.

Hands were covered in gloves or lace mittens and handbags were made of velvet and silks, decorated with needlework or beads.

Very young boys and girls dressed so alike that it was difficult to tell them apart. Both wore dresses over ankle-length pantaloons. Older boys wore sailor suits which remained the fashion for many years. The older girls copied their mothers, but with shorter dresses.

Unlike women's clothes men's fashions did not change dramatically. Gradually by 1860, men lost the romantic dash and individuality of colour of the early 1800s, becoming heavier with the arrival of the dark unimaginative woollen frock coat, which, accompanied by a plain waistcoat, was only slightly relieved by the coloured, checked or striped trousers without creases or turnups.

A simple form of bow tie replaced the elegant cravat worn over a starched, pleated shirt.

Hair was fairly long, parted in the centre or side and brushed forward to curl over the ears with side whiskers, sometimes accompanied by a moustache. Country hats for men were low crowned and broad brimmed. The essential tall, cylindrical top hat, of silk or felt, in fawn, grey or black, completed the town gentleman's wardrobe.

Leather shoes and boots, tended to be narrow in the foot and square at the toe, often with gaiters.

The clothes for men and women of this period, although lacking in originality and imagination, gave an impression of reassuring dependability similar to the rich drapes and stuffy hangings which were crammed into the parlours and sitting rooms; this heavy claustrophobic extravagance was reflected in the formal clothes of the time.

1860

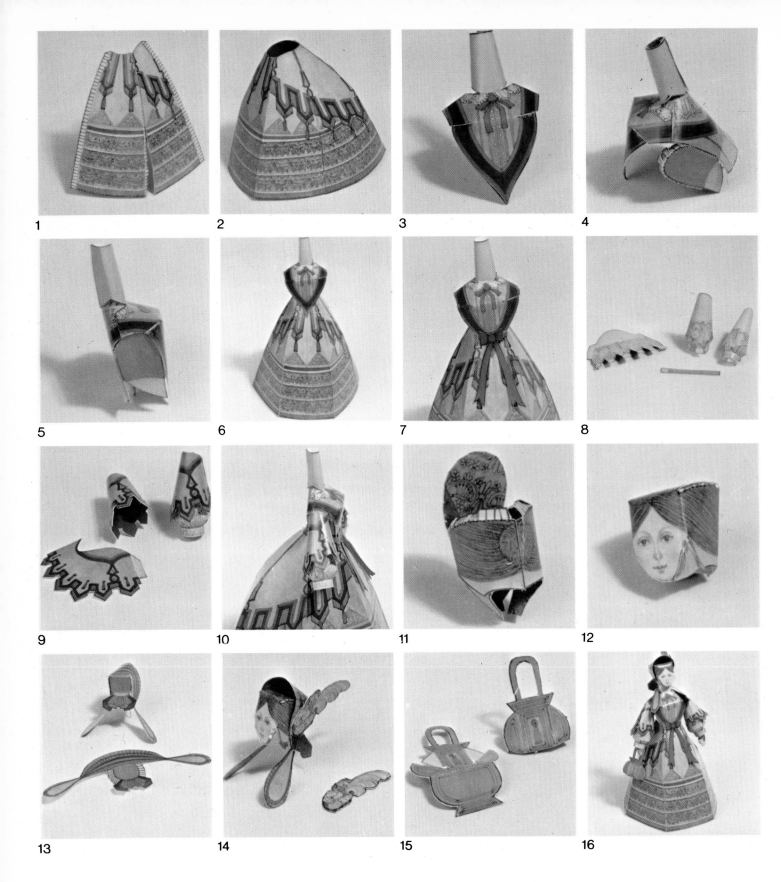

1 2 3 4

5 6 7 8

9 10 11 12

13 14 15 16

On the next two pages you will find a costume model of 1860
Cut out the pages carefully along the cutting lines.
When making the model it is important to follow the assembly
order by numbers as shown above.

For general instructions on cutting, folding and glueing see
page 4.

On the back of the cutout pages there are patchwork patterns.
These form the patterned linings to the dresses, hats and ribbons etc.

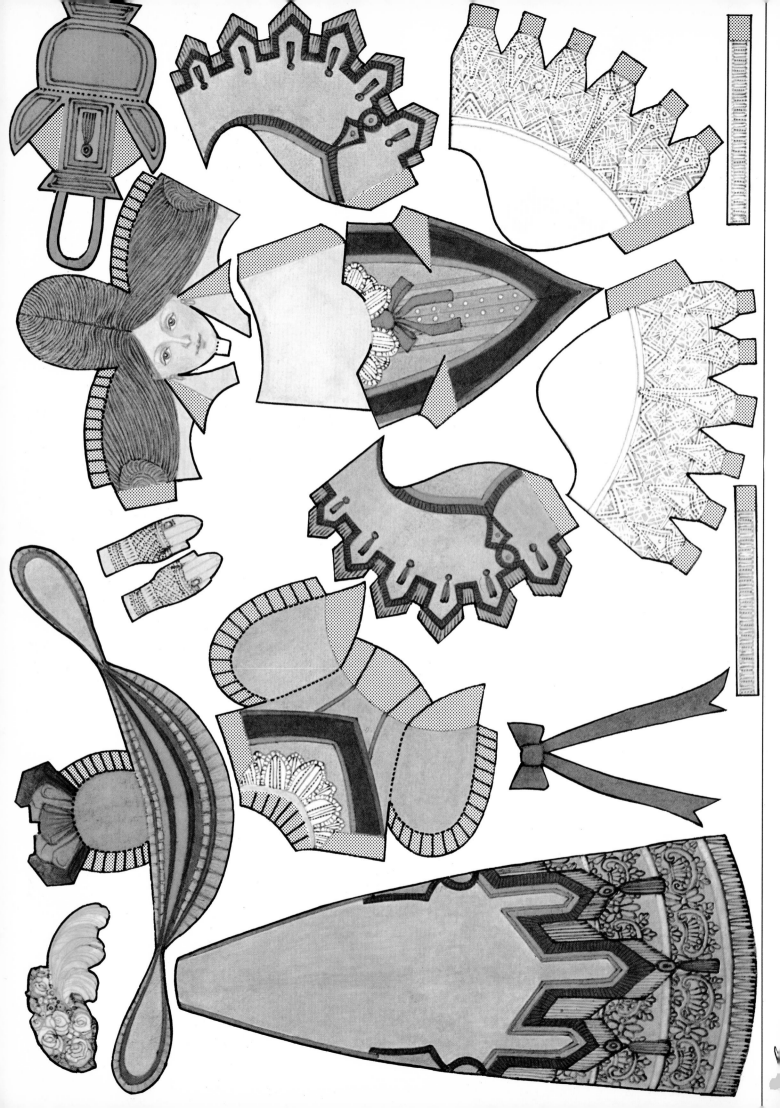

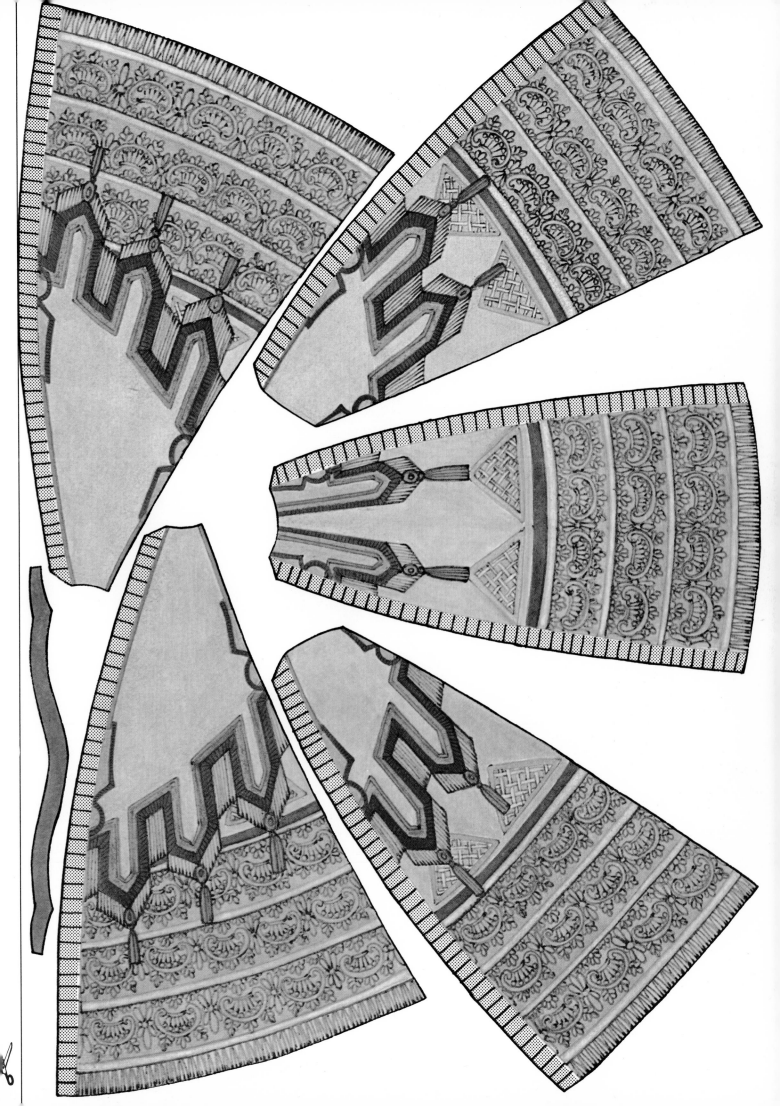

1865

1868

1870

1875

8 Fashion magazines with illustrations of the latest modes made it not only possible for all women to follow the latest styles, but also to choose patterns for themselves, thus expressing their individual personalities.

By 1867 it was recorded that America was manufacturing two hundred thousand sewing machines each year for the world market and with the introduction of these time-and-labour-saving devices, the ready-to-wear clothing industry grew rapidly, although ladies of society still ordered their dresses from the dressmakers. However, a young Englishman, Charles Worth, who worked in Paris, had the new idea of preparing a collection of dresses to offer his customers and the first Haute Couture fashion house of Paris was born. Paris collections showing complete ensembles, assured French supremacy over women's clothes throughout the world; Paris dictated the fashion and everyone followed.

The crinoline had grown larger and larger until, like most extremes of fashion, it became ridiculous—and with lighted candles and gas lamps—highly dangerous as it was so easy for the huge skirts to catch fire. After a few modifications, such as a half crinoline called a crinolette, it finally disappeared from favour by 1870 and it then became as important to reveal the shape of the female figure as it had been to conceal it under the mushrooming crinoline. Women's hips, previously hidden from view, came back into sight as the skirts were draped closely around the body and then bunched up behind over a 'dress improver'—a boned half-cage which supported the back of the skirt, so that the material fell from it into a long train which swept the floor. The skirt, looped up and back, was adorned with frills, ribbons and flounces. The half-cage was soon replaced by the small jaunty 'bustle' which jutted out from the lower back and was made of rolls of braided wire in a stuffed cushion shape tied around the waist by tapes. The

feminine shape under the sweeping gown was further enhanced and shown off to advantage by a stylish tight-fitting tailor-made jacket with long tight sleeves, the tiny waist emphasised by a line of buttons down the front. The back of the jacket sat on top of the bustle, with the skirt flowing down to the ground in a great many flounces.

For wealthy society women it was important to dress according to the occasion. Clothes for the morning and afternoon, clothes for formal dinners, and clothes for the theatre. Rich shot-silks, taffetas, satins, delightful striped or checked patterned cottons and linen were all used to subtle effect. Glossy and dull materials were mixed together and draped into pleats and swags in the same dress. Day dresses, with the introduction of the newly-discovered aniline dyes, were garish in bright hues such as royal blue, emerald green, cerise and plum.

For evening wear white was still predominant, with gowns cut daringly low and square at the bosom, with short sleeves.

Hair, like the dresses, was drawn back and piled high in a chignon, or bun, on top of the head with falling loops and twists of hair hanging down to the shoulders. Small perky hats were worn well forward over the forehead in a great variety of styles, decorated with feathers, lace, flowers or ribbons. For the evening the hair was entwined with sprays of flowers, ribbon streamers or jewelled clasps.

Precious stones in heavy, ornate settings were fashionable jewellery, and at night close-fitting necklaces encircled the delicate throat, with large matching earrings almost reaching the shoulders. During the day short silk or kid gloves protected the pale hands, and the fashionably fair skin was shielded from the sun's rays by a long-handled parasol.

Brocaded slippers, often with small heels, were worn indoors. High heeled boots, laced up in front or buttoned at the side were worn out of doors.

Women could now take up simple sports. Free at last from the cumbersome clumsiness of the swaying crinoline their clothes took on a lively, pretty and pert appearance helped by the bewitching twitch of the bustle and the figure-flattering jackets.

Essentially men's fashions became simplified, for evening wear the cut-away coat was necessary and for morning wear a coat with the front sloping away at the sides was to remain in fashion for many years. However, the single or double-breasted frock coat, shaped at the waist and fully buttoned, in fawn, greys or black was considered correct for town.

Trousers were light in colour, in plain greys or striped, fitting the legs loosely, but narrowing slightly below the knees. A new informality was creeping into men's dress by the introduction of the short jacket, the ancestor of the modern jacket and for daytime a starched round collar was worn with a cravat, or the less formal turned down collar with a knotted or bow tie.

With the growing interest in various sporting activities it was necessary to wear more comfortable clothes. A craze for bicycling initiated a strange outfit consisting of a jacket in checked rough material with matching 'knickerbockers' stopping just below the knee. Thick woollen stockings filled in the gap between the knickerbockers and the black or brown ankle boots, which were sometimes topped with leather gaiters. Men of this era felt undressed without a hat, during daytime and for evening wear. For visits to town the top hat was essential with the frock coat, although the low crowned black or fawn bowler hat (or 'Derby' as it is called in America), with the brim slightly curved up at the sides was becoming fashionable. The sporting version of the bowler was covered in tweed material, soft caps of similar fabrics were popular, and the deerstalker with peaks at front and back was worn for fishing and shooting.

For evening a black tail-coat was worn with a front pleated white shirt, short white waistcoat and white bow tie.

Hair was cut quite short and parted in the middle or side. Side whiskers and moustaches helped the young men to look older and more responsible, whilst the older men strived to look like wise sages, under large beards. Inconspicuous jewellery was acceptable, being confined to a gold ring and perhaps a gold watch and chain, as well as a tie pin set with jewels, gold cuff links and shirt studs set with pearls or diamonds.

The tremendous progress in the manufacture of superb cloths, both plain and woven, enabled men and women to take pride in the cut and quality of their clothes, and to possess a selection for different occasions, ranging from theatre going to roller skating.

1875

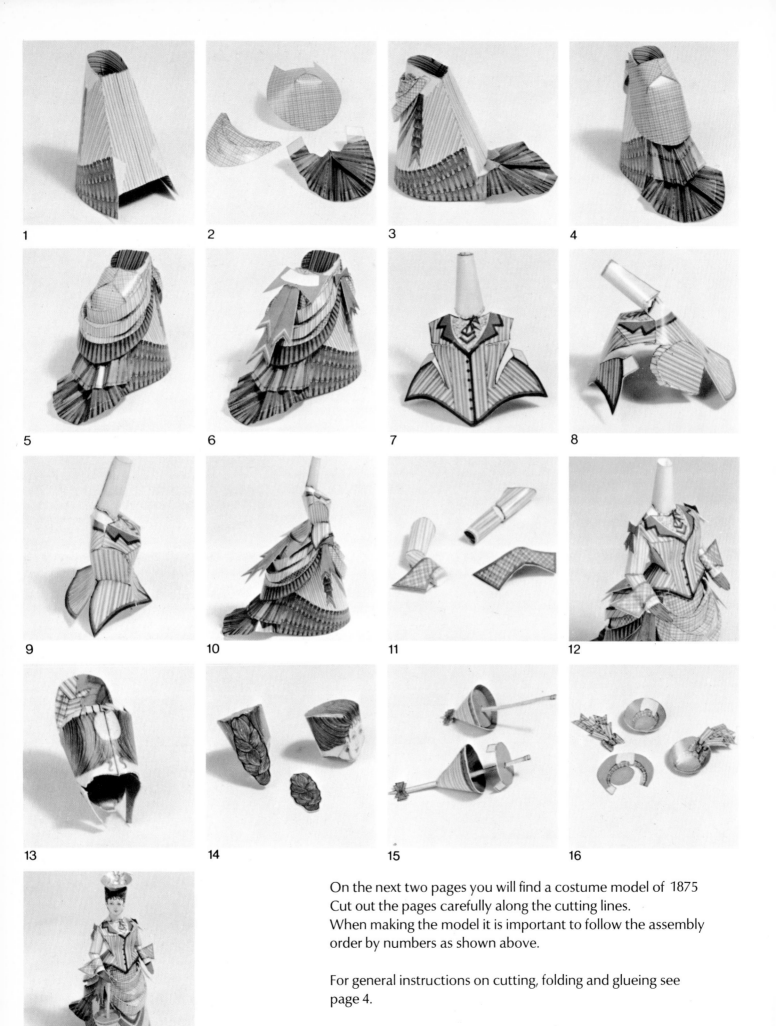

1

2

3

4

5

6

7

8

9

10

11

12

13

14

15

16

17

On the next two pages you will find a costume model of 1875
Cut out the pages carefully along the cutting lines.
When making the model it is important to follow the assembly
order by numbers as shown above.

For general instructions on cutting, folding and glueing see
page 4.

On the back of the cutout pages there are patchwork patterns.
These form the patterned linings to the dresses, hats and ribbons etc.

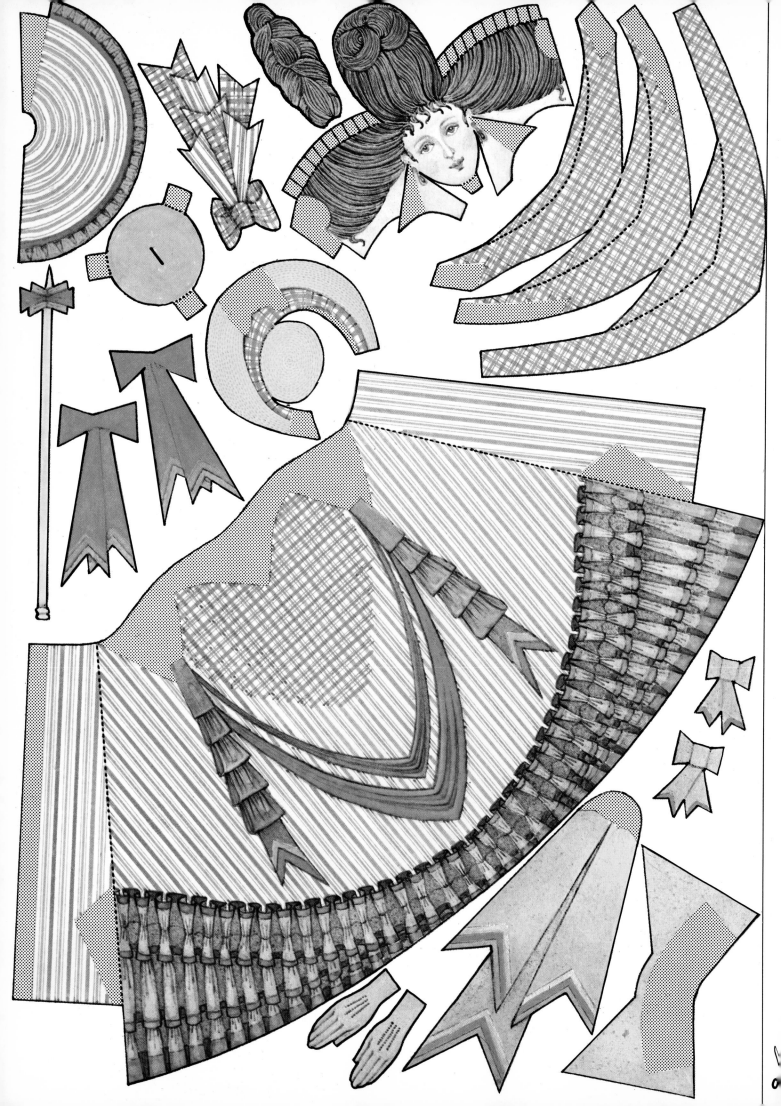

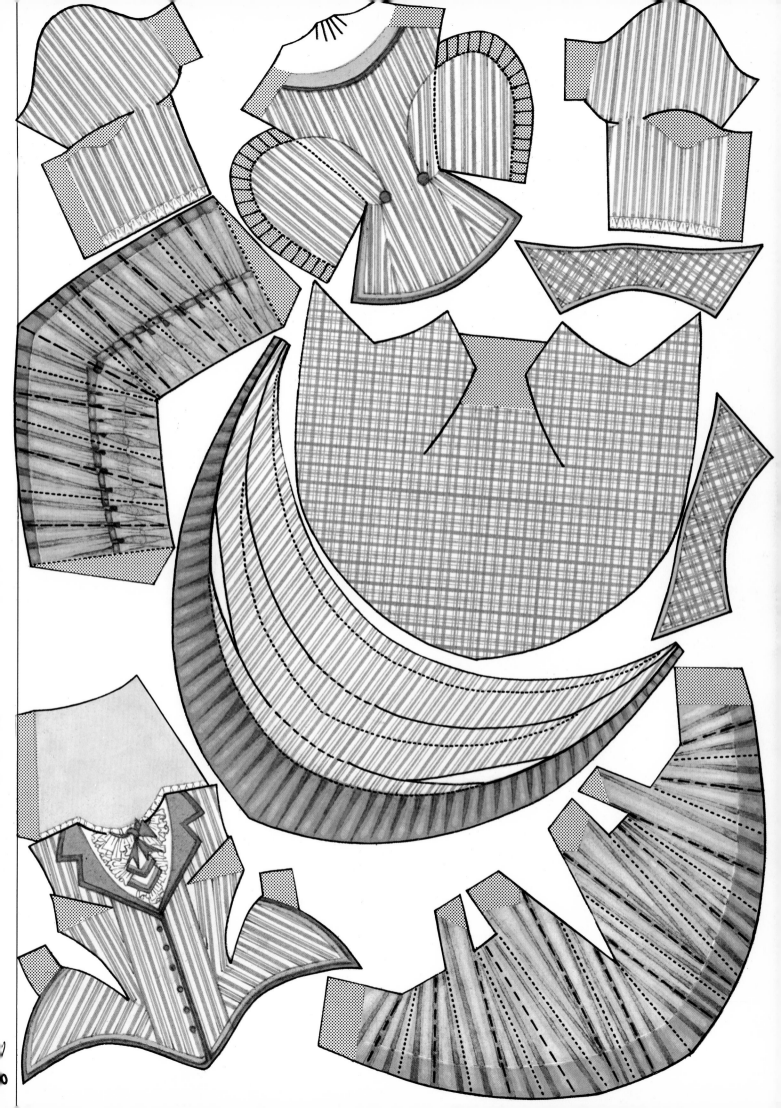

1895

1878

1885

1900

1905

9 The bustle grew higher and larger until by 1887 it gained truly exaggerated dimensions. Then it disappeared, although the waist was still kept small by the well tailored and boned seams of the bodice. During the daytime the collar remained high with abundant trimmings of lace. 'Gigot', or leg-of-mutton, sleeves were puffed out at the shoulder narrowing to a tight fit from the elbow to the wrist.

Towards the end of the 1800s a new practical dress was now worn by the young women earning their livings as typists and shop assistants. Close fitting, tailored, hip length jackets, were worn over elaborate blouses with either a high lace collar, or a stiff masculine collar and tie, with a long flared, simply cut, ground length skirt, tightly belted at the narrow waist allowing the blouse to pouch out over it. The whole effect gave a crisp clean line suitable for the informality of games and sports such as archery, tennis, croquet, skating or bicycling.

The Wright Brothers flew their first aeroplane in 1903, and the cinema was opening up a new world to everybody. Materials became soft and clinging, the flowing lines of the gowns harmonizing with the twisting curving flowing lines of the Art Nouveau style in decorative art. Chiffon, tulle, linen, muslin, and voile were made into attractive dresses and the more expensive natural subtle coloured silks, satins, brocades and velvets, lavishly outlined with lace, minute tucks, tiny beads, miniature buttons and narrow ribbons, were in great demand by elegant society women.

Delicate hues and gentle pastel shades were all the rage for blouses, coats and skirts in light pink, blue, green and yellow, light brown or grey. Although at the same time, French couturiers influenced by the costume designs for the Russian ballet, preferred the bold contrasts of brilliant exotic oriental colours.

These highly sophisticated gowns demanded exaggerated curves, achieved by the new foundation garment which

moulded the figure into a curious S shape, by pushing the bust forward over a tiny waist; the back arched inwards at the waistline and the stomach was flattened. The women of fashion had to look heavy in the bust and rear, so padded corsets helped enormously.

The tightly belted trumpet shaped skirt was composed of sections flaring outwards at the hem, making it necessary to lift the skirt daringly when out walking, showing the flounces of the petticoat.

The blouse was high-necked with a deep lace yoke and high collar boned at the sides to stand up round the neck with a satin or silk neckband.

With the aids of pads, combs, slides and hair pins the hair was piled on top of the head in a bun with a loose upward sweep. The front arranged softly in puffs and waves made a foundation for the vast hats, perched high on the head, laden with ostrich feathers and flowers and anchored in place by means of a long elaborate hat pin. It was still not considered proper for a lady to wear more than the slightest suspicion of make-up.

Daytime accessories consisted of vanity bags, long handled parasols, and large muffs in winter. Long feathered boas fluttered round the lace collared necks and long kid or silk gloves were worn outdoors during daytime or with evening dress.

The cool sophisticated, wealthy woman with her wardrobe of outfits for every occasion, was equally matched by the men. Men's formal dress had altered little, although the black morning suit was now more fashionable with the jacket bound at the edges with silk, worn with dark striped or checked trousers. The man's short dinner jacket was first worn at this time for comfort during the long evenings. The new fashion for ironing a crease down each trouser leg did away with the baggy unkempt look. The short jacket of the lounge suit with a slit in the back became universal and was worn with matching trousers.

For motoring through the countryside gentlemen wore tweed Norfolk jackets with broad pleats at the back and a wide belt above large pockets, with knee breeches. Stiff cuffs and starched upright, or turned-down, collars with bow or knotted tie were obligatory, but when boating or bicycling during the heat of the summer, the light summer suit kept the wearer cool.

Although silk top hats remained in favour, bowler hats were common. The new straw boater or straw panama with a silk band brightened the summer days, while sporting tweed hats kept the head warm in the winter countryside. Hair was quite short at the back and sides and brushed backwards usually with a centre parting. Beards were worn by elderly men, but the young man was clean shaven, apart from a moustache trimmed in a variety of styles.

Laced, polished black or brown, leather boots were changed in summer for white buckskin or canvas boots or shoes. Elegance demanded few masculine accessories, a silver topped cane, a simple tie pin, and a pair of gloves completed the gentleman's wardrobe.

From 1905 onwards faster transport and speedy means of communication appeared to reduce the size of the world, and women's fashion was to become more uniformally international. The American influence of the hobble skirt followed in 1910—with the new craze for dancing tangos. Later in the 1920s the Charleston brought in the age of the Flapper. Never before had girls worn waistless, knee length skirts nor dared to cut their hair quite so short, and tight corsets were abandoned altogether.

There were gradual adjustments in the styles for men who began to wear the lounge suits more and more. These have only changed in cut to become more casual and relaxed during recent years.

During and after the Second World War women learnt to wear utilitarian, masculine styles with padded high shoulders and trousers became gradually acceptable wear.

Fashion has always changed whenever a style had been pushed to an extreme. Just as panniers and hoops gave way to sheath dresses, so the masculine clothes became more feminine with the more romantic 'new look' after the Second World War. Skirts, pullovers, suits and dresses continued to be modified and changed in cut, without any really startling variation, until in the 1960s skirt hems shot up, and nearly vanished with the mini skirt. Having gone so far, down it came again! Perhaps the greatest fashion change of all in present times is the lack of any real definite style to follow. Most people now wear exactly what they please to suit the contemporary scene.

1905

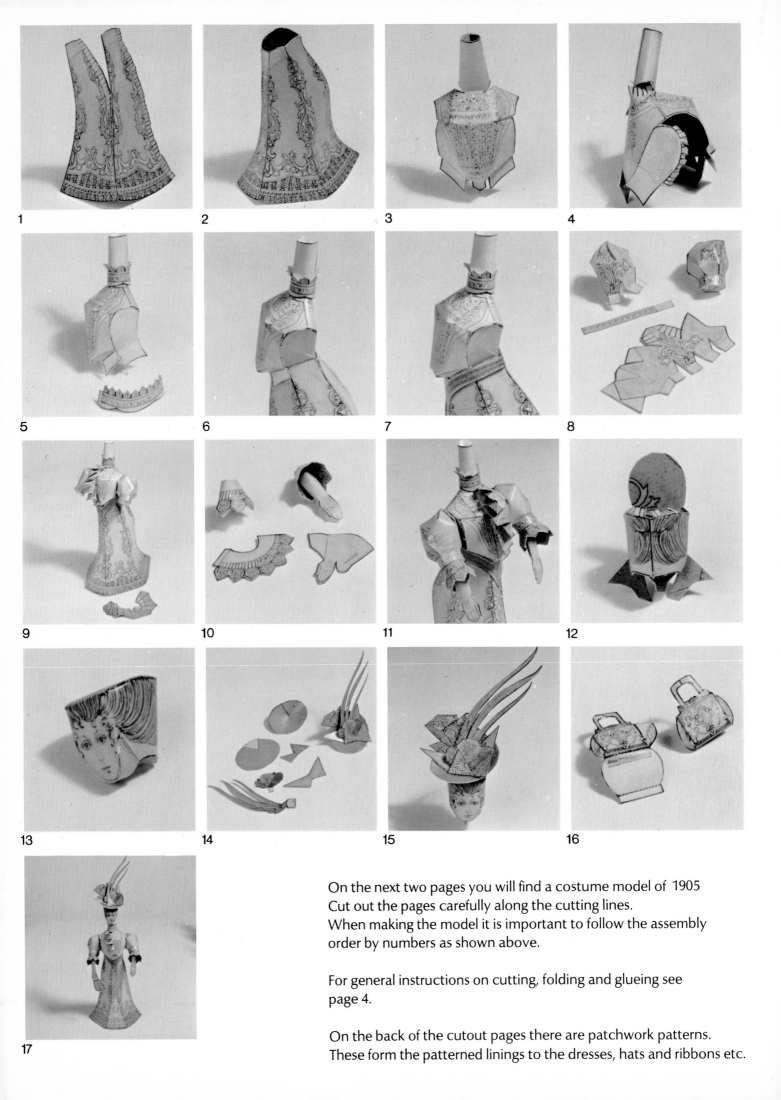

1

2

3

4

5

6

7

8

9

10

11

12

13

14

15

16

17

On the next two pages you will find a costume model of 1905
Cut out the pages carefully along the cutting lines.
When making the model it is important to follow the assembly
order by numbers as shown above.

For general instructions on cutting, folding and glueing see
page 4.

On the back of the cutout pages there are patchwork patterns.
These form the patterned linings to the dresses, hats and ribbons etc.

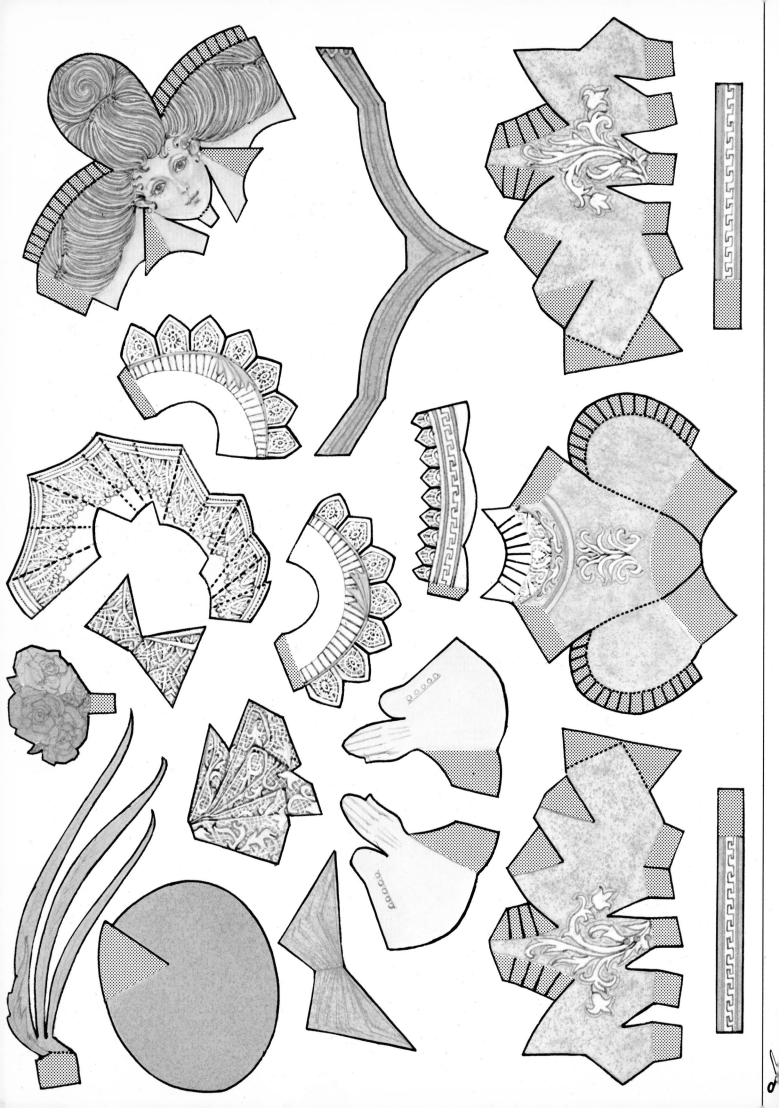

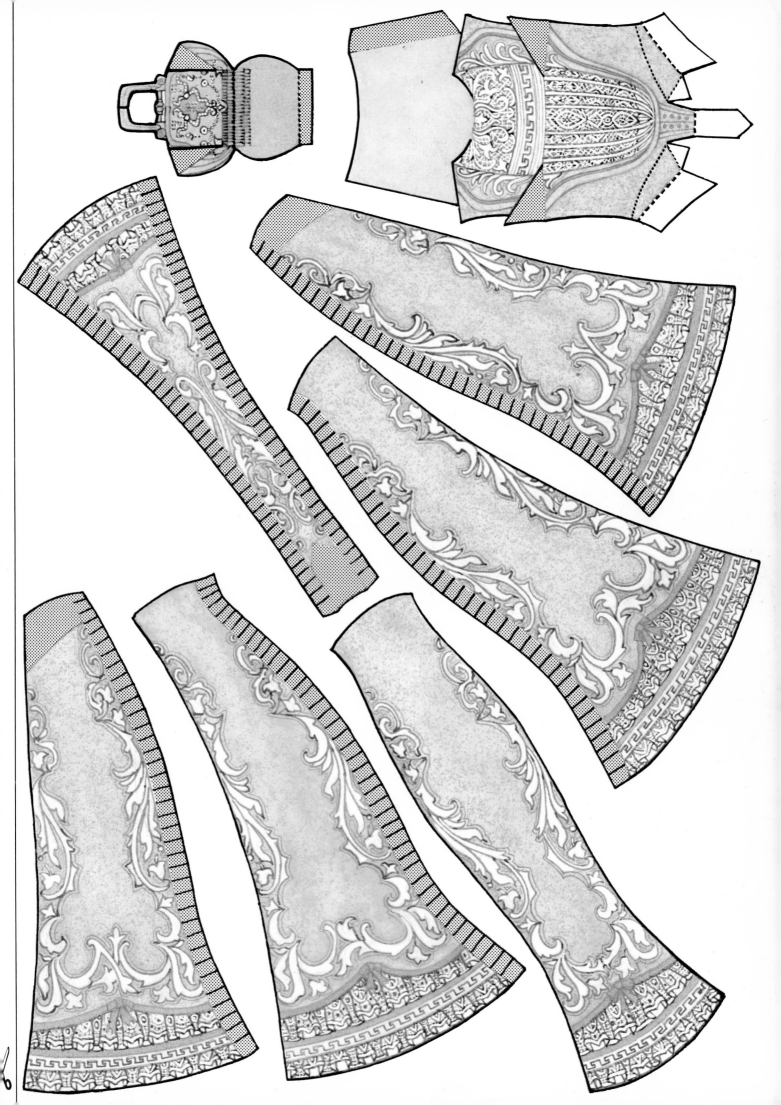

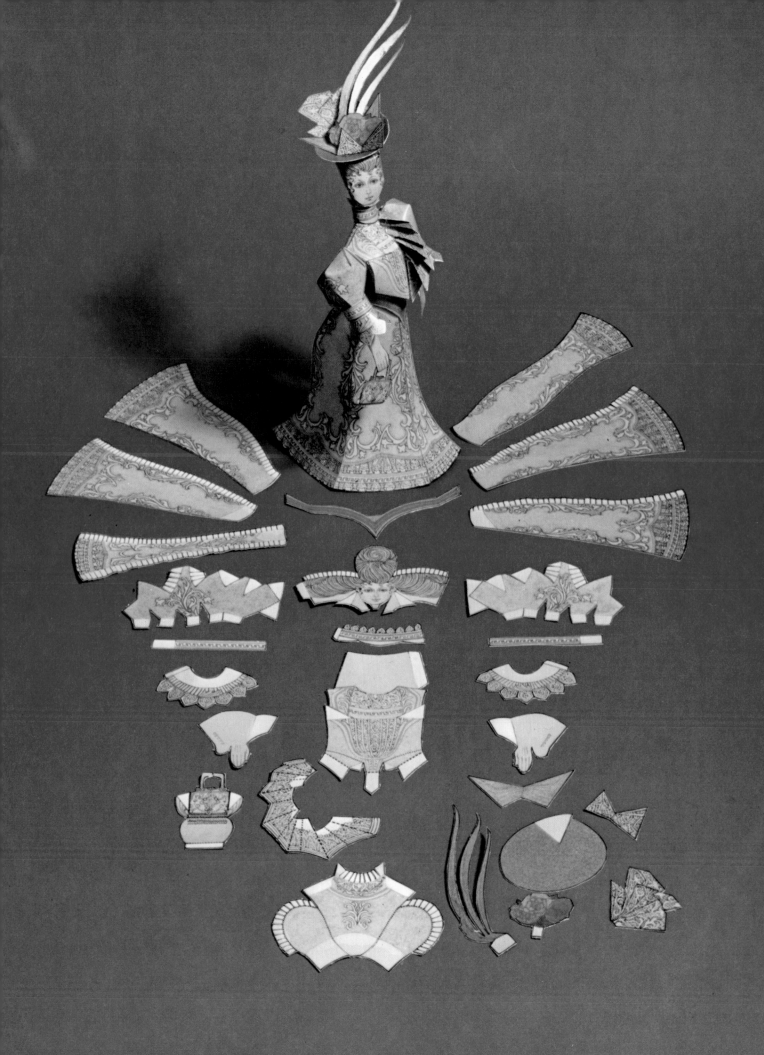

When you have made the models and their backgrounds.

Cut out the booklet pages carefully along the black line. Punch holes at intervals along the margin, bind with metal rings, or thread ribbon, loosely tied, through the holes.

Cut out each fashion plate carefully along the black line. Pin them on the wall or else paste them first onto a coloured background as shown.

You will now have a complete costume collection of your own.

Special thanks are due to Trevor Jones and Diana Hall for all their help, and to Donald Southern for all the photographs.
R. L. and C. K.